Dressing
Porcelain
Dolls

Maxine Henry

First published in the United States of America in 1996
by the Chilton Book Company, Radnor, Pennsylvannia

©Maxine Henry 1995

ISBN 0-8019-8870-5

Printed in Singapore

Originally published in Great Britain in 1995 by
B. T. Batsford Ltd
4 Fitzhardinge Street
London W1H 0AH

Line drawings by Deborah Matthews and Maxine Henry
Photographs by Sue Atkinson

With thanks to my friend Joan,
who introduced me to the world of dolls

CONTENTS

PORCELAIN DOLLS IN HISTORY

Miniature replicas of the human form have been made in a wide variety of materials almost since humans inhabited the earth. It is not clear when the early images, which were used as religious idols, became playthings. One of the earliest dolls, discovered in an ancient tomb in Rome, dates back to between AD 150 and 160. It is exquisitely carved in ivory and has a shapely jointed body and an elaborately carved hairstyle.

Throughout the centuries, dolls have reflected the period in which they were made, both in the type of manufacturing materials used and in the style of their costuming. We can learn much about social and industrial progress through the study of dolls and their fashions. The development of the doll progressed from ivory and bone, and by the mediaeval period dolls were being manufactured from terracotta, wood and cloth. It is interesting to note that many centuries later, after progressing through wax, papier-mâché, composition, porcelain, celluloid and vinyl, we still make dolls in wood and cloth and there has been, in recent years, a growing interest in reproducing porcelain dolls from the 1850-1930 period.

Dolls play a special part in the life of a child. A doll will often become a confidant, a comforter and an outlet for the child's affections. A firm attachment can be formed between a child and a doll, which often lasts a lifetime, and of all the child's toys it is the doll which is usually the favourite. It becomes a much-loved member of the family.

Porcelain dolls These can be divided into three main types – china, Parian and bisque.

China dolls Glazed china dolls date from the early 1800s and have a glossy appearance. German factories which normally manufactured porcelain tableware began to produce dolls. Many were sold as heads only, the bodies being made up at home, so the shape and size of these dolls varied considerably.

The hair was moulded and painted in a vast variety of ornate styles. The early dolls had black or brown hair but on later dolls blonde was introduced. The faces were beautifully painted and the china quality of the early dolls was very good.

Most of these dolls were produced in Germany and later, from 1850, in France, when the shape and style changed. The majority of the French dolls were sold on commercially produced bodies similar to the later French fashion dolls.

Parian dolls These dolls were made from a white unglazed porcelain resembling marble from the Greek island, Paros, hence their name. They are easily identified by their painted features, pale faces and rosy cheeks. They were made in Germany from 1850 to 1880, and the workmanship and painting were of a very high standard.

Bisque dolls Dolls were made of bisque, a type of very fine unglazed porcelain, from 1850 onwards. France produced a wide variety of beautiful bisque dolls which were noted for their quality and expressive, well-moulded features. There were numerous French factories producing dolls during this period, but Jumeau and Bru were perhaps the most famous of all the French doll-makers.

Bisque dolls were highly prized and expensive to buy. The early dolls were fashion dolls, replicas of adults, but by the late 1890s bébé dolls, dolls which represented children, became popular. Bisque dolls often had pierced ears and sometimes hair eyelashes. In 1855 beautiful threaded, handblown glass eyes were introduced, replacing the previous painted ones. The dolls came on a variety of bodies, from inexpensive wire calico, gusseted kid and composition to more expensive all-bisque bodies. Most dolls produced were girl or lady dolls – only about 10 per cent were boy dolls. French doll-making started declining around 1895 because Germany was producing high-quality porcelain dolls at cheaper prices, dominating the market worldwide. The heyday of German doll-making lasted from 1850-1930 and was destroyed by the recession between the two world wars.

Many of these beautiful dolls have survived and command prohibitively high prices. There is, however, a growing interest in reproducing French and German dolls from this period, not as children's playthings but as exquisitely dressed ornaments.

THE CLOTHES

The dolls' clothes in this book are based on fashions from the second half of the nineteenth century – particularly the extravagantly luxurious dresses of the rich. During this period the Industrial Revolution and mechanisation brought sweeping changes in lifestyles and subsequently in fashions. The sewing machine was invented around the 1850s and completely changed the fashion industry.

One of the most noteworthy names associated with fashion is Charles Frederick Worth (1825-95), an Englishman who left London to work in a Paris fashion accessory shop. He later married a shop girl who encouraged him to design fashion garments. In 1858 he founded *haute couture* in Paris. His reputation was enhanced by the Empress Eugenie, wife of the French Emperor Napoleon III. She favoured his designs and his success spread across the whole of Europe. During this period the textile industry began manufacturing a wide variety of sumptuous materials and this, together with the Empress's love of luxury fabrics for dresses, made Paris the fashion centre of Europe.

Later, fashion garments were copied and mass produced, making them reasonably priced and available to all. Many of the garments made from these luxury fabrics could not be washed, but dry cleaning was available from the 1870s. Too much cleaning spoilt the fabrics so stains were removed by spot cleaning with gin! Underarm dress preservers were used from 1840 and perfumed sachets from 1865.

It was in 1856 that the first synthetic dyes were discovered by the English scientist Sir William Perkin (1838-1907) while he was trying to synthesise quinine. He was knighted in 1906 for his discovery of mauve. These new dyes had a dramatic effect on the fashion industry.

As you can see, an interest in dolls provides a microcosm of the era.

For instructions on making the dress at the front of the rail (left), see page 20.

GENERAL INSTRUCTIONS

Outfits and patterns All the outfits in this book are suitable for dressing antique or reproduction dolls. They are arranged in order of doll height beginning with the smallest doll, Gloria. She measures 38cm (15in). The largest, Noelle, measures 56cm (22in).

Star ratings The patterns have been star rated to show the standard of sewing skills required.
* indicates that the pattern is very simple to sew.
** indicates that the pattern is suitable for an average sewer.
*** indicates that the pattern is a little more complicated than * and **.

Sewing tips

Fabrics Where possible, use natural fabrics for the dolls' clothes, e.g. silk, cotton lawn, silk satin, taffeta, fine wool and cotton lace. The choice of colour and fabric is important. Even if the style is correct for the period, brightly coloured modern fabrics will not give an authentic look to your doll.

Stitching The clothes have been made up using a sewing machine but, because they are so tiny, they could easily be hand stitched. If you are dressing a reproduction of an antique doll using a machine, work French seams or neaten flat seams by turning over a small hem and straight stitching, or overcasting by hand – the facility to zigzag is too modern for authenticity. You may also, for this reason, prefer to hand embroider on the garments rather than use machine embroidery.

If you are machining the clothes, use a shorter stitch length than normal and a fine needle.

Pressing A small travelling iron and a sleeve board make pressing easier. Press each seam immediately after sewing for a better finish.

Patterns Check your doll's measurements as heads and body shapes vary, and adjust the pattern pieces accordingly.

Trace off the patterns from the book. To avoid pin-marking the fabric, cut out the pattern pieces in paper, place them on the fabric and draw round each piece with tailor's chalk or an air-soluble pen. The shape may then be cut out without the risk of pin marks.

Mark braid placement lines and notches on the fabric with dressmaker's carbon paper.

The seam allowance on all pattern pieces is 0.5cm (¼in). This may seem rather narrow if you are used to making full-size garments. If you wish to make up the garments using French seams, remember to allow a wider seam allowance.

Check that your doll's feet will fit the shoe pattern. Stand your doll on a piece

Abbreviations

r.s. = right side
w.s. = wrong side
r.s.f. = right sides facing
w.s.f. = wrong sides facing

Knitting abbreviations

st = stitch
sts = stitches
inc = increase
st.st. = stocking stitch
(1 row k,1 row p)
tog = together
k = knit
p = purl
sl = slip
sl1 = slip one stitch
psso = pass slipped stitch over
yf = yarn forward
yon = yarn over needle
rep = repeat

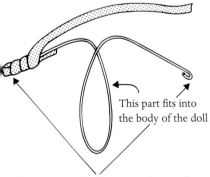

The two cut ends of wire are bent to form loops which are bound with wadding and pushed into the porcelain arms

of paper and draw around one foot. Cut out the paper shape. The sole pattern in the book should be slightly larger than your cut-out shape; this allows for the thickness of the socks.

Making instructions – diagrams Working diagrams are included for some instructions, and are indicated at the beginning of the instructions – (Ga), (Gb) for Gloria's outfit, (Ba), (Bb) for Bernadette's, and so on.

Fastenings Press studs were not invented until well after the beginning of the twentieth century. To be authentic when dressing earlier reproduction dolls, use buttons (not plastic ones) and hooks and eyes.

Small buttonholes are difficult to sew neatly. You may find it easier to hand sew small loops to fasten the buttons.

Much of the underwear of the period was fastened with tape or ribbon.

Dyeing Since it is difficult to buy cotton lace in many colours, it may need to be dyed. Fabric paints are inexpensive and easy to use. They give an 'antique' finish to the lace and you can mix the exact depth of colour you require. Always let the lace hang free while drying, to avoid the colour being patchy. Pressing with a hot iron will make the colour permanent. Use tea or coffee (without milk!) to dye white lace and fabric cream. Always try a small sample first.

In the nineteenth century, beer was used to dye the lace cream; this also produced a starched effect.

Car spray touch-up paint can be useful for colouring shoes, fans, bags, etc to match your doll's outfit.

Trimmings Frequent jumble sales and antique markets for old lace, trimmings, ribbons, feathers, buttons, etc. Old hatpins, small buckles, brooches and earrings often give just the right look to an outfit.

Underwear Much of the underwear of this period was made from fine cotton lawn or flannel. However, it was made of silk for outfits requiring a touch of luxury.

Instructions for a wired calico body

A loop of wire is inserted into the doll's body. The ends of the loop pass down the doll's arms, allowing them to bend and stay posed rather than hanging limply at the sides of the body.

Cut a length of wire (from a wire coathanger, for example) long enough to extend from one arm across to the other arm plus 20cm (8in).

Bend the armature to the shape shown in the diagram and bind it with a strip of wadding.

Insert the loop into the doll's body while you are stuffing it.

Stuff the porcelain forearms three-quarters full with tissue paper. Insert the ends of the armature into the arm and push well up into the porcelain forearms.

Continue stuffing the doll until the body is firm.

GLORIA

Christening layette

This doll is a porcelain reproduction of the 1920s Armand Marseille doll, Gloria. She has porcelain hands, a head with a flange neck and a soft-jointed body. All the fabric and the lace for this outfit was dyed using a tea bag in boiling water to obtain an 'antique' look. Scraps of fabric and lace were tested for the required density of colour before dyeing the fabric used for the outfit. Gloria's outfit consists of dress, bonnet, petticoat, pilch, vest and bootees. The bonnet, dress and petticoat bodices, pilch, vest and bootees are lined.

Dimensions

Height: 38cm (15in)

Circumference of head: 28cm (11in)

Waist: 30cm (12in)

Neck: 19cm (7½in)

Pattern pieces There are 19 pattern pieces for Gloria's entire outfit, numbered G1 to G19 and printed on pages 21-25.

Christening dress ★★

The dress has a self-lined, back-fastening bodice which has two lace-edged frills over the shoulders. The bodice front is decorated with pin tucks, embroidery, beads and lace. The skirt is full and long and the hem is edged with a lace-trimmed frill. The decorated sleeves fasten with ribbon at the wrists.

Materials and notions

1.10m (43in) fine cotton lawn 150cm (60in) wide – this is also sufficient for the bonnet, the pilch and the bootees
5m (196in) cotton scalloped braid 1.5cm (⅝in) wide
4m (158in) insertion lace 2cm (¾in) wide
5m (196in) narrow ribbon for insertion lace and bows
1.35m (53in) cotton lace 3.5cm (1⅜in) wide
75cm (29½in) cotton lace 2.5cm (1in) wide
Small pearl beads
Sewing threads to match
Machine or hand embroidery threads (optional)
Four tiny mother-of-pearl buttons
Strips of till roll paper or stitch-and-tear Vilene if you are embroidering by machine

Pattern pieces There are six pattern pieces for the christening dress, numbered G1 to G6.

Sewing tips

For authenticity, you may wish to embroider and tuck the bodice by hand. If you prefer to work on the machine, follow these instructions.

Cut an oblong of fabric slightly larger than the bodice front pattern. Work the decoration and then cut the bodice front to size. The dress bodice has a machine embroidery stitch of tiny leaves, sewn down the centre, using a shiny embroidery thread. To prevent the fabric puckering whilst the machine embroidery is in progress, place a strip of till roll paper or stitch-and-tear Vilene under the fabric, and tear it off the back when the design is completed.

Using a double needle and tightening the top tension, work two rows of pin tucks down either side of the leaves. Use a wing needle, and till roll on the back of the fabric, for the row of honeycomb stitches on either side of the pin tucks.

Complete the panel with another row of pin tucks sewn on either side. Decorate the skirt front by sewing two parallel rows of tiny leaves down the centre front, again using till roll. Sew another two rows 20cm (8in) to the left of the central panel, and another two rows 20cm (8in) to the right of the central panel. Also embroider two parallel rows of leaves down the centre of the sleeves from shoulder to wrist. These, and the leaves on the bodice front, are decorated with tiny pearl beads.

Thread narrow ribbon through the insertion lace (except the lace which is used for the sleeve bottoms as this needs a longer length of ribbon) before sewing up.

Making instructions

1 Work all embroidery and pin tucks.
2 With r.s.f., join shoulder seams on the dress bodice. Press. Repeat with the bodice lining.

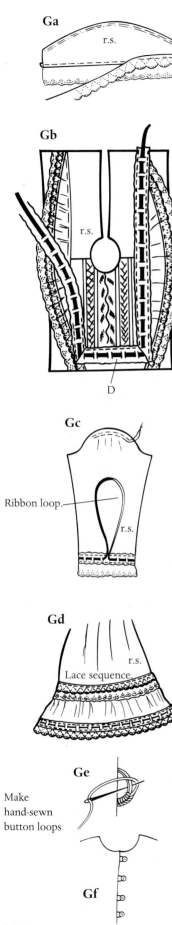

Ga

r.s.

Gb

r.s.

D

Gc

Ribbon loop.

r.s.

Gd

r.s.

Lace sequence.

Ge

Make
hand-sewn
button loops

Gf

3 Neaten the straight raw edge of both shoulder frills. Turn up a small single hem 0.5cm (¼in) and straight stitch in place.

4 Sew a row of narrow cotton lace to the hem and then a row of scalloped braid to overlap the lace.

5 (Ga) Gather the curved edge of the frills by sewing two rows of long straight stitches. Pull up the gathers so the frill fits the bodice. It should extend from the front waistline up over the shoulders down to the back waistline.

6 Tack and sew the frills to the right side of the bodice, placing the gathered edge along the placement line marked on the pattern.

7 (Gb) Cover the gathered edge of the frill with insertion lace, sewing up the back, over the shoulder, down the front and across the front at the waist, pleating the corners as you go, back up the other side of the front, covering the gathered edge of the second frill, and over the shoulder finishing at the back waist edge. The insertion lace is stitched flat along both edges except at D (the front waist edge) where only the top edge of the insertion lace is stitched.

8 Gather the sleeve heading.

9 At the wrist edge of the sleeve, turn over a small single hem, 0.5cm (¼in) wide, to the right side of the fabric and straight stitch in place.

10 Cover the hem with a row of narrow lace.

11 (Gc) Sew a length of insertion lace at the sleeve edge just above the row of lace, leaving a loop of ribbon at the centre of the sleeve to cut and tie in a bow.

12 With r.s.f., sew sleeve heading into armhole. Repeat.

13 With r.s.f., sew up the side seam and down the sleeve seam. Repeat with the other side and press.

14 With r.s.f., sew the bodice to the bodice lining, up centre back opening, around neck and down centre back opening. Clip curves, turn to right side and press.

15 Sew bodice lining side seams.

16 Turn under a narrow hem and hand sew lining armhole to bodice armhole.

17 R.s.f., seam the two skirt frill pieces together to form a circle.

18 Neaten the bottom edge of the frill.

19 Turn a 0.5cm (¼in) hem to the w.s.and straight stitch in place.

20 Sew a row of scalloped braid on the r.s. along the bottom edge of the frill.

21 Sew a row of insertion lace just overlapping the top of the braid.

23 R.s.f., sew up the back skirt seam leaving an 8cm (3in) opening at the waist edge. Press.

24 Gather the top edge of the frill to fit the bottom edge of the skirt. With r.s.f., sew frill in place.

25 (Gd) Press the seam towards the waist of the skirt and sew a row of flat, wide cotton lace on the r.s. of the skirt just above the seam line. The bottom edge of the lace hangs down over the gathers of the frill. Sew a row of scalloped cotton braid just above the lace.

26 Gather the waist edge of the skirt to fit the waist of the dress bodice leaving a small overlap on the bodice for fastening. With r.s.f., sew skirt to bodice, taking care not to catch the bodice lining or the bottom edge of the insertion lace.

27 (Ge) (Gf) Sew four buttons to bodice back as indicated on pattern and sew button loops to correspond on the other edge.

28 Decorate the bodice and sleeves with tiny pearl beads and the bottom of the skirt with small ribbon bows.

Bonnet ★★

The bonnet has a back of ruched cotton lawn, a lace crown and a gathered lace frill. The gathered lace frill is starched – use spray starch or fabric stiffener.

Materials and notions

70cm (27½in) cotton lawn 15cm (6in) wide – there is sufficient fabric for the bonnet in the measurement given for the dress (page 12).
85cm (33⅓in) cotton lace 5cm (2in) wide – 60cm (24in) of this is stiffened and used for the bonnet frill
26cm (10in) scalloped cotton braid
Three small ribbon bows
1.5m (59in) transparent ribbon 2.5cm (1in) wide
12cm (4¾in) insertion lace
Sewing thread to match

Pattern pieces There are four pattern pieces for the bonnet, numbered G7 to G10.

Making instructions

1 (Gg) Sew scalloped edging to the bonnet crown following placement line on the pattern.
2 (Gh) To make the bonnet frill, gather the remainder of the wide lace, and pull up evenly to fit the curved edge of the bonnet crown. Using the previous row of stitching as a guide, and with r.s.f., sew the bonnet frill to the bonnet crown along the curved edge.
3 (Gi) Gather the bonnet back along the nine gathering lines indicated on the pattern. Pull up the gathers to fit the doll's head. Optional: stitch rows of embroidery across alternate gathered lines, using till roll paper or stitch-and-tear Vilene behind the embroidery.
4 Stitch a row of gathers between Xs and pull up evenly to fit crown.
5 R.s.f., sew back of bonnet to back of crown.
6 Gather bonnet lining as indicated and pull up to fit bonnet back.
7 R.s.f., stitch bonnet back to bonnet lining through all layers, taking care not to catch the top edge of the frill, and leaving neck edge open for turning.
8 Turn to the right side and, with r.s.f., stitch bonnet neckband in place.
9 Turn neckband to the inside of the bonnet, fold under the raw edge and slip stitch in place by hand, leaving the ends open.
10 (Gj) Thread the ribbon through the neckband.
11 Optional: hand sew a short length of insertion lace to cover the neckband.
12 (Gk) Stitch the three small bows in place, one at each end of the neckband and one in the centre of the bonnet crown.
   Note: If the front edge of the lace crown gapes, run a row of gathers along the edge and pull up to fit the doll's head.

Gg

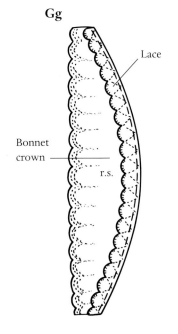

Lace

Bonnet crown

r.s.

Gh

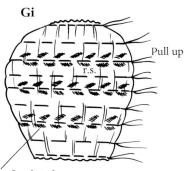

Gathered frill

r.s.

Face edge

Gi

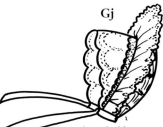

Pull up

r.s.

Leaf embroidery

Gj

Thread ribbon ties through neckband

Gk

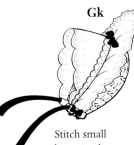

Stitch small bows in place

Petticoat ★★

The petticoat bodice is self lined and the front is overlaid with cotton lace fabric. The skirt is gathered onto the bodice and has three tucks at the hemline. The hem is finished with a cotton scalloped braid and has a row of insertion lace above the tucks. The bodice is fastened at the back with tiny hooks and eyes.

Materials and notions

1m (39in) fine lawn or cotton 150cm (60in) wide – this is also sufficient for lining the bootees
11cm (4½in) cotton lace 18cm (7in) wide to cover the bodice (optional)
1.25m (49in) insertion lace and ribbon
1.25m (49in) cotton scalloped braid
Three small hooks and eyes
Sewing thread to match

Pattern pieces There are three pattern pieces for the petticoat, numbered G11 to G13.

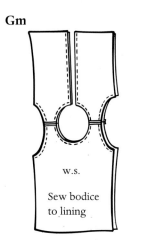
Tack lace overlay in place

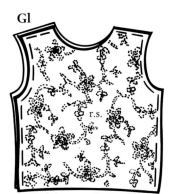
Sew bodice to lining

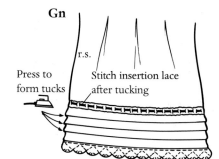
Press to form tucks   Stitch insertion lace after tucking

Making instructions

1 (Gl) Tack lace overlay to bodice front.
2 R.s.f., join bodice shoulder seams. Press open.
3 Repeat with the lining.
4 (Gm) R.s.f., sew bodice to bodice lining up one back opening, around neck and down the other back opening. Sew around armholes leaving side seams open. Clip seams.
5 Turn bodice to right side by pulling the backs through the shoulders.
6 R.s.f., join lining side seam, sew across armhole and down bodice side seam. Repeat with the other side. Press.
7 Sew the centre back seam of the skirt leaving an 8cm (3in) opening at the waist edge. Neaten and press the seam open.
8 Neaten the bottom edge of the skirt and turn up a narrow 0.5cm (¼in) hem.
   Sew a row of scalloped braid along the hem line.
9 (Gn) Measure 4cm (1½in) from the hem and press to form the bottom tuck.
10 (Gn) Sew a row of stitching 1cm (½in) from the pressed fold.
11 (Gn) Press the fold down towards the hem. Measure 2cm (1in) from the line of stitching and press a second fold.
12 (Gn) Sew a row of stitching 1cm (½in) from the second pressed fold.
13 (Gn) Press the second fold downwards towards the hem to make the second tuck.
14 (Gn) Measure 2cm (1in) from the second row of stitching and press a third fold.
15 (Gn) Sew a row of stitching 1cm (½in) from the third pressed fold and press downwards to form the third tuck.
16 (Gn) Stitch a row of insertion lace along the top of the tucks.
17 Sew two rows of gathering threads around the waist edge of the skirt and pull up evenly to fit the bodice leaving a small overlap on the bodice for fastening.
18 R.s.f., sew the skirt to the bodice taking care not to catch the bodice lining.
19 Turn under a narrow hem and slip stitch the bodice lining in place by hand enclosing the gathered edge of the skirt.
20 Hand stitch the hooks and eyes to the bodice back.

Pilch ★★

The pilch is lined with flannelette or towelling and fastens at the front with ties and buttons.

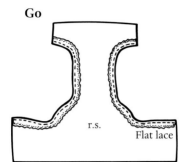

Go

Materials and notions
28cm (11in) cotton lawn 40cm (16in) wide – there is sufficient fabric for the pilch in the measurement given for the dress (page 12)
28cm (11in) flannelette or fine towelling 40cm (16in) wide
Two small buttons
60cm (24in) very narrow cotton lace
90cm (35½in) narrow tape 0.5cm (¼in) wide
Sewing thread to match

r.s.
Flat lace

Pattern pieces There is one pattern piece for the pilch, marked G14.

Making instructions
1 (Go) R.s.f., stitch lace at leg openings along placement line, with straight edge of lace to raw edge of fabric.
2 R.s.f. and enclosing the lace, stitch the lining to the pilch all around the edge, leaving openings as marked on the pattern for the tape and for turning to the right side.
3 Clip corners and curves, turn to the right side and press.
4 Slip stitch by hand the opening left for turning.
5 Make two small buttonholes as marked on the pattern.
6 Sew a line of stitching through both layers to make a casing for the tape as indicated on the pattern.
7 Thread tape through the casing.
8 (Gp) Fit the pilch on the doll and mark the position for the buttons.
9 Attach two tape ties at ★.
10 An optional row of embroidery can be sewn between the buttonholes.

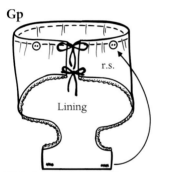

Gp

r.s.

Lining

Pilch showing tapes and buttons

Vest★

The vest is made from fine wool lined with cotton lawn. It wraps over at the front and is fastened with ribbon ties. It is decorated with two lace motifs.

Materials and notions
20cm (8in) fine wool 40cm (16in) wide
20cm (8in) cotton lawn 40cm (16in) wide
60cm (24in) ribbon 2mm (⅛in) wide
Two lace motifs – the motifs in the photograph (page 19) were cut from a piece of lace
Sewing thread to match

Pattern pieces There are two pattern pieces for the vest, numbered G15 and G16.

Making instructions
1 R.s.f., join the vest shoulder seams. Press.
2 Repeat with the lining.
3 Tack the ties in place on the righthand front.
4 (Gq) With r.s.f., sew the vest to the lining up the front, around the neck and back down the other front, taking care not to catch the free ends of the ties in the seam. Sew the vest to the lining around the armholes.

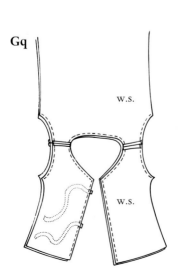

Gq

w.s.

w.s.

Gr

5 Clip seams and turn the vest to the right side by pulling the fronts through the shoulders.

6 With r.s.f., and armhole seams matching, sew up the vest side seams across the armhole seams and down the lining side seams. Press.

7 Press a small hem to the w.s. at the bottom of the vest and press a small hem up on the lining. Stitch the hems together enclosing the raw edges.

8 (Gr) Sew the lefthand ties in place and sew the two motifs to the front.

Bootees *

The bootees are lined and have a quilted sole. The fronts are overlaid with lace and decorated with small pearls and a ribbon bow. Optional: hand stitch a row of very narrow cotton lace around the top.

Leg and foot sizes vary, so check that the pattern fits your doll.

Materials and notions

10cm (4in) lawn 60cm (24in) wide – there is sufficient fabric for the bootees in the measurement given for the dress (page 12)

10cm (4in) lining 60cm (24in) wide – there is sufficient lining fabric for the bootees in the amount given for the petticoat (page 16)

10cm (4in) lace fabric 10cm (4in) wide for overlays

30cm (12in) narrow cotton lace (optional)

Fourteen small pearl beads

A small scrap of wadding for the soles

Sewing thread to match

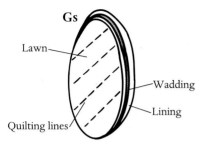

Gs
Lawn
Wadding
Lining
Quilting lines

Gt
w.s.
Heel dart

Pattern pieces There are three pattern pieces for the bootees, numbered G17 to G19.

Making instructions

1 (Gs) R.s.f. uppermost, make a sandwich with the soles: lawn, wadding, lining. Quilt diagonal lines through all layers.
2 With r.s.f., match A and B on bootee upper and seam together.
3 (Gt) Stitch back heel dart.
4 Repeat Instructions 2 and 3 with the lining.
5 Tack lace over bootee front and, r.s.f., stitch front to bootee upper matching notches. Turn to r.s.
6 Repeat with lining, omitting lace.
7 With r.s.f., stitch lining to bootee around the top edge, turn to the right side.
8 (Gu) From the inside of the bootee stitch the sole to the upper through all layers, matching notches to dart and seam. Neaten raw edge.
9 (Gv) Turn to the right side and decorate the front lace panel with small pearl beads. Attach a small bow on the lace panel at X. Hand stitch lace around the bootee top.
10 Repeat Instructions 1-9 with the second bootee.

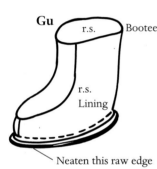

Gu
r.s. Bootee
r.s. Lining
Neaten this raw edge

Gv
Small pearl beads

An additional dress to fit a 38cm (15in) tall doll
The dress pattern for Gloria can be adapted to make the dress photographed on the front of the clothes rail on page 6.

The bodice has been lengthened by 17cm (6½in) and the skirt is shorter, measuring 19cm (7½in) from the waist to hem. The sleeves are cut slightly narrower and have a puffed overlay. These can be cut by cutting out two additional sleeve tops 5cm (2in) wider that the sleeve pattern and 6.5cm (2½in) shorter at the wrist edge. (To sew the puffed sleeves, see page 31, Instructions 4-6.) The skirt has a gathered lace overlay, the lower sleeves have a lace overlay and the bodice has a lace 'V' on the front. A sash, gathered at intervals, is sewn round the dropped waistline. Small ribbon roses decorate the sleeves and bodice front.

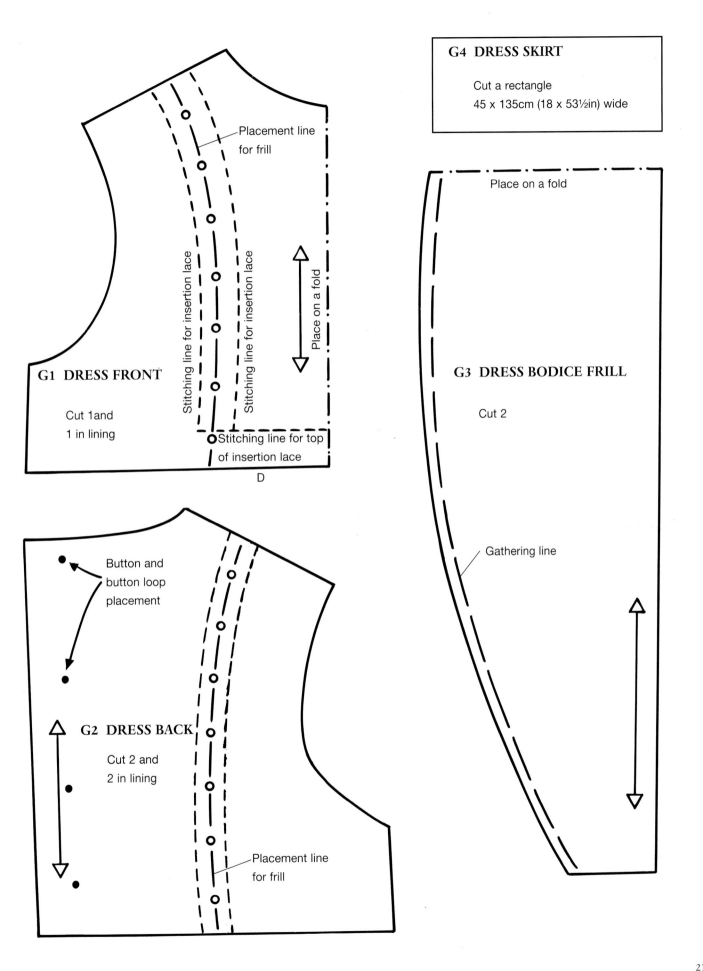

G1 DRESS FRONT

Cut 1and
1 in lining

Placement line
for frill

Stitching line for insertion lace

Stitching line for insertion lace

Place on a fold

Stitching line for top
of insertion lace

D

G2 DRESS BACK

Cut 2 and
2 in lining

Button and
button loop
placement

Placement line
for frill

G4 DRESS SKIRT

Cut a rectangle
45 x 135cm (18 x 53½in) wide

Place on a fold

G3 DRESS BODICE FRILL

Cut 2

Gathering line

21

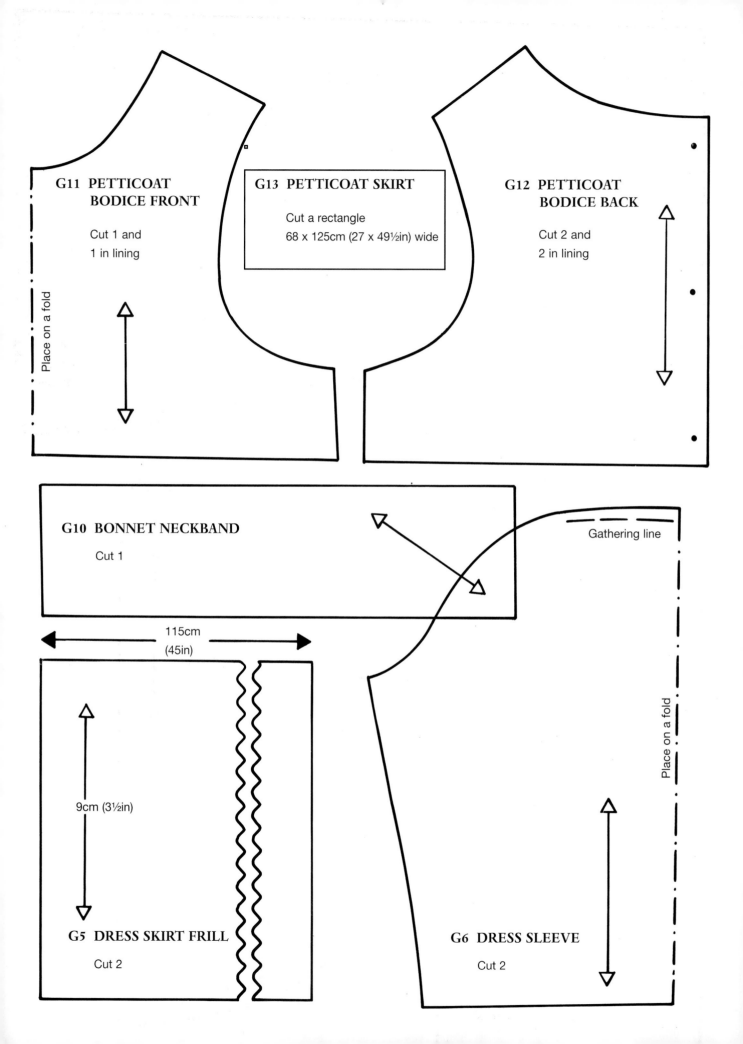

G11 PETTICOAT BODICE FRONT

Cut 1 and
1 in lining

Place on a fold

G13 PETTICOAT SKIRT

Cut a rectangle
68 x 125cm (27 x 49½in) wide

G12 PETTICOAT BODICE BACK

Cut 2 and
2 in lining

G10 BONNET NECKBAND

Cut 1

Gathering line

Place on a fold

115cm
(45in)

9cm (3½in)

G5 DRESS SKIRT FRILL

Cut 2

G6 DRESS SLEEVE

Cut 2

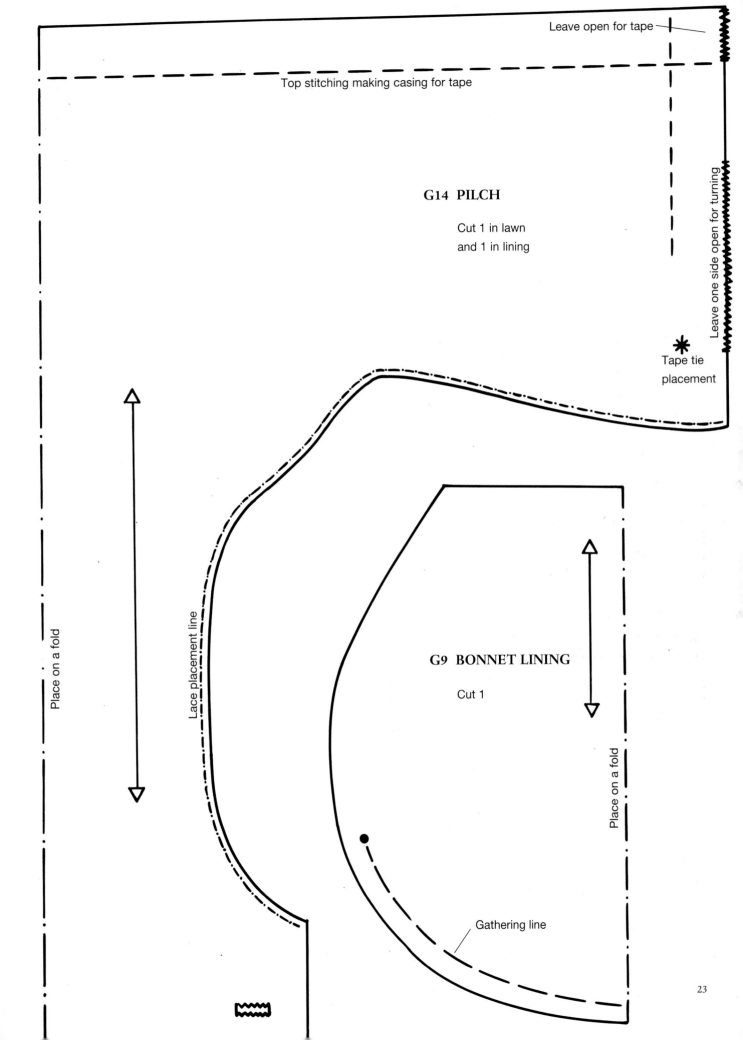

Leave open for tape

Top stitching making casing for tape

G14 PILCH

Cut 1 in lawn
and 1 in lining

Leave one side open for turning

✳
Tape tie
placement

Place on a fold

Lace placement line

G9 BONNET LINING

Cut 1

Place on a fold

Gathering line

23

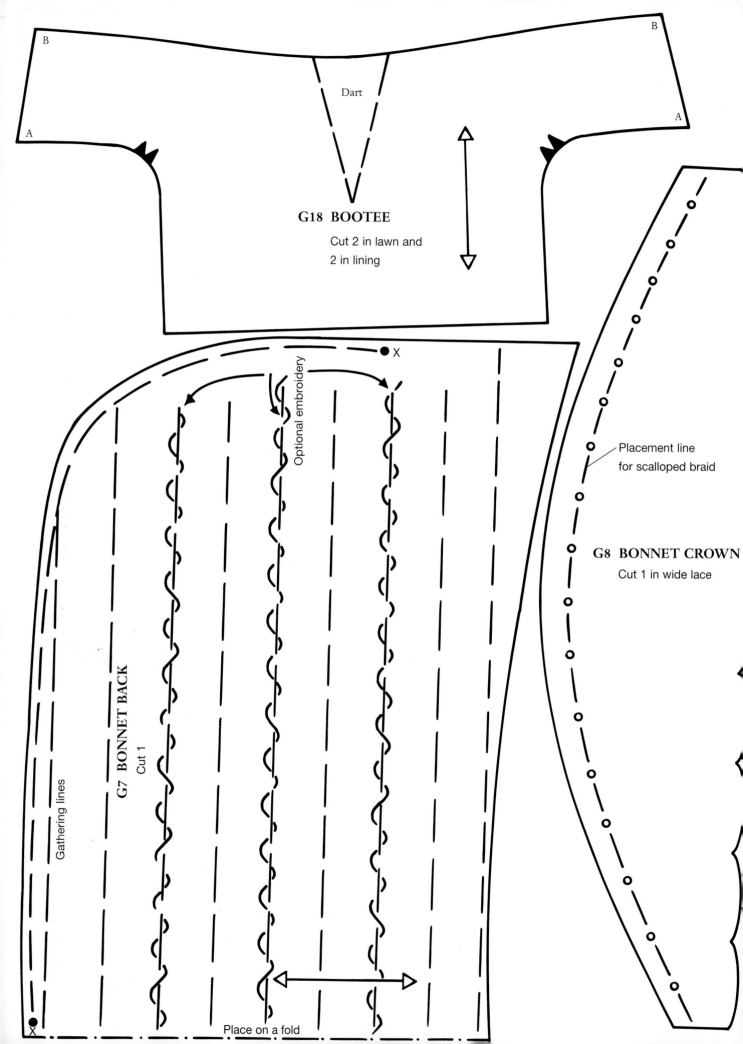

G18 BOOTEE

Cut 2 in lawn and
2 in lining

Dart

B

B

A

A

X

Optional embroidery

Placement line
for scalloped braid

G8 BONNET CROWN

Cut 1 in wide lace

G7 BONNET BACK

Cut 1

Gathering lines

X

Place on a fold

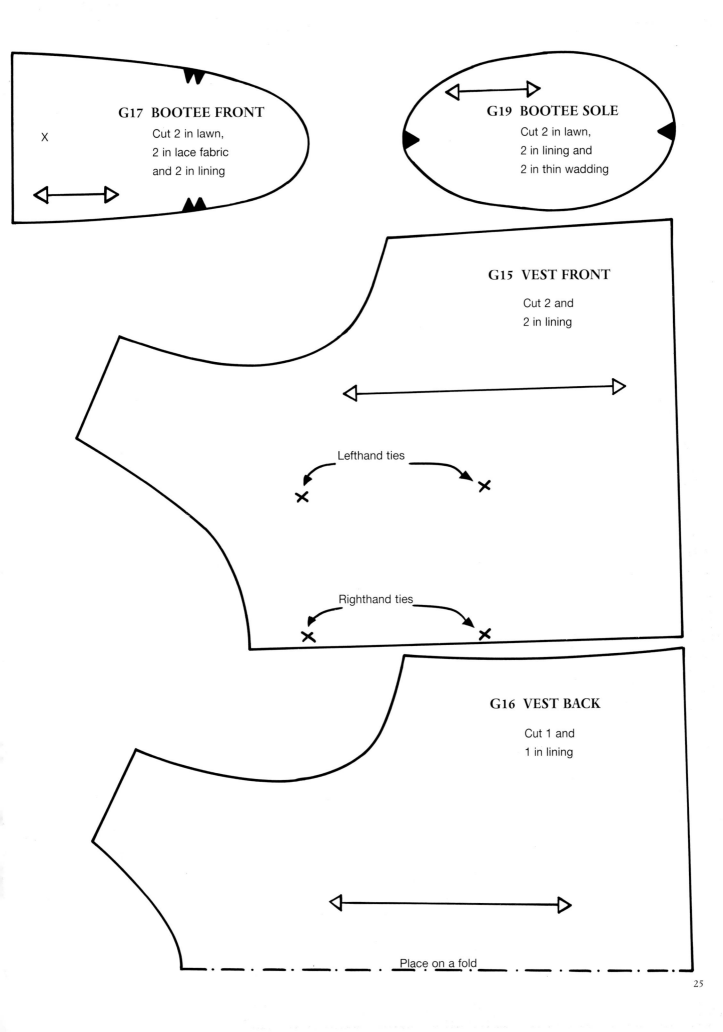

G17 BOOTEE FRONT

X

Cut 2 in lawn,
2 in lace fabric
and 2 in lining

G19 BOOTEE SOLE

Cut 2 in lawn,
2 in lining and
2 in thin wadding

G15 VEST FRONT

Cut 2 and
2 in lining

Lefthand ties

Righthand ties

G16 VEST BACK

Cut 1 and
1 in lining

Place on a fold

25

RENÉE

Ball gown

This doll is a reproduction of a French fashion doll. The original doll was unmarked but is attributed to the Jumeau factory. She has a porcelain head, shoulder plate, lower arms and lower legs, glass paperweight eyes and a calico body with wired arms (see page 9).

The dress has a gathered skirt with a beaded lace overlay and a separate close-fitting bodice. The idea for the design was taken from a photograph of the singer Jenny Lind. Renée's outfit consists of skirt, bow, bodice, evening bag, petticoat, cage crinoline, corset, split leg combinations and shoes. The skirt has an overskirt, the bodice, corset and combinations are self-lined, and the evening bag is lined.

Dimensions

Height: 39cm (15½in)

Circumference of head: 20cm (8in)

Waist: 15cm (6in) – the waist in the finished outfit is smaller

because this doll wears a corset

Neck: 11cm (4½in)

Pattern pieces There are 25 pattern pieces for Renée's entire outfit, numbered R1 to R25 and printed on pages 38-43.

Skirt★★

The back-fastening skirt has three frills cascading around the hem and a bead-embroidered lace overskirt. The skirt back is decorated with a large velvet-trimmed bow.

Materials and notions
30cm (12in) dupion silk 115cm (45in) wide
32cm (12½in) taffeta 90cm (35½in) wide
90cm (35½in) cotton lace 20cm (8in) wide – several rows of narrower lace may be sewn together to make this width
3.5m (138in) narrow cotton lace
Sewing threads to match
Small beads
One hook and eye

Pattern pieces There are three pattern pieces for the skirt, numbered R1 to R3.

Making instructions

1 Turn up a very narrow hem along the edge of a frill and attach a length of narrow lace to this small hem. With r.s.f., seam together the two short edges of the frill.

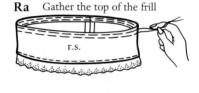

Ra Gather the top of the frill
r.s.

2 (Ra) Turn a narrow hem to the w.s. along the top of the frill and run two rows of gathering threads along this hem.

3 Repeat with the other two frills.

4 With r.s.f., sew up the back seam of the skirt leaving an 8cm (3in) opening at the waist edge. Turn up and sew a narrow hem to the w.s. at the bottom of the skirt. Press.

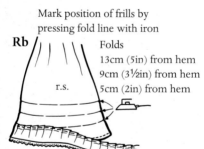

Mark position of frills by pressing fold line with iron

Rb Folds
13cm (5in) from hem
9cm (3½in) from hem
5cm (2in) from hem
r.s.

Sew frills around bottom of skirt on fold lines

5 (Rb) Pull up the frills to fit the width of the skirt and with the w.s. of the frill against the r.s. of the skirt sew the first frill around the bottom of the skirt 5cm (2in) above the hem. It is easier to keep the frill straight if you iron a crease 5cm (2in) above the hem and line up the frill with this crease while sewing it in place.

6 (Rb) Repeat this with the other two frills, sewing the second frill 9cm (3½in) above the hem and the third frill 13cm (5in) above the hem.

7 Sew up the back seam of the lace overskirt again leaving an opening at the waist edge, and trim close to the seam.

8 (Rc) Fit the overskirt over the main skirt matching the back openings. With the top raw edges level sew two rows of gathering stitches at the waist edge. Pull up the gathers to fit the doll's waist leaving a flat area across the front section.

9 With r.s.f., stitch the waistband to the skirt top, turn to the wrong side, turn under a narrow hem and hand stitch in place.

10 Neaten the back opening and sew a hook and eye to the waistband.

11 Decorate the lace with small beads. You may find it easier to sew the beads following the pattern on the lace.

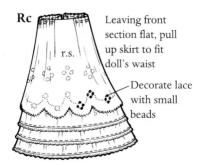

Rc Leaving front section flat, pull up skirt to fit doll's waist
r.s.
Decorate lace with small beads

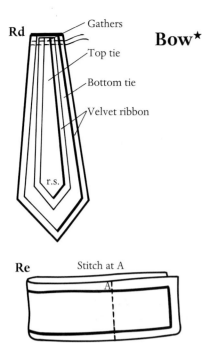

Rd Gathers — Top tie — Bottom tie — Velvet ribbon — r.s.

Bow★

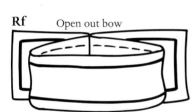

Re Stitch at A — A

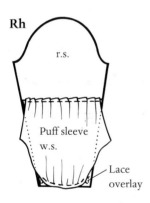

Rf Open out bow

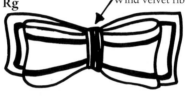

Rg — Wind velvet ribbon round centre of bow

Materials and notions

Silk dupion – there is sufficient fabric for the bow in the measurement given for the bodice (below)
2m (79in) very narrow velvet ribbon

Pattern pieces There are three pattern pieces for the bow, numbered R4 to R6.

Making instructions

1 With r.s.f., seam the two bottom tie pieces together leaving the edge opposite the point open for turning. Repeat with the other tie. Clip, turn and press.
2 Stitch narrow velvet ribbon around ties on placement lines.
3 (Rd) Fold in a narrow hem at the top of the ties, gather and stitch together.
4 Fold the bow in half lengthways and, with the r.s.f., seam round the bow leaving an opening for turning. Clip, turn and press.
5 (Re) Sew velvet ribbon as indicated, fold the bow in half and stitch a row of stitching at A.
6 (Rf) Open out the bow so that the stitching lies at the centre back of the bow.
7 (Rg) Make the bow knot by winding velvet ribbon round the centre of the bow, hand stitch at the back and catch stitch to the top of the ties.
8 Stitch the bow to the back of the skirt at the waist.

Bodice★★

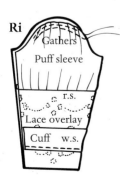

Rh r.s. — Puff sleeve w.s. — Lace overlay

Ri Gathers — Puff sleeve — r.s. — Lace overlay — Cuff w.s.

The back-fastening, self-lined fitted bodice has a bead-embroidered lace overlay on the front panel. There is a frill of gathered lace around the low square neckline, the armholes and waist are also edged with frilled lace.

Materials and notions

30cm (12in) silk dupion 115cm (45in) wide
20cm (8in) taffeta 115cm (45in) wide
30cm (12in) lace 10cm (4in) deep
1.40m (54in) narrow lace
20cm (8in) very narrow velvet ribbon
Beads and sequins
Sewing thread to match
Five hooks and eyes
Five small jet beads

Pattern pieces There are six pattern pieces for the bodice, numbered R7 to R12.

Making instructions

1 Tack the lace overlay to the bodice front.
2 Sew all the darts on the bodice and bodice lining, press towards the side seams. You may require only one set of darts on the bodice back – check your doll's waist measurements.
3 With r.s.f., sew the bodice front to the side fronts matching the notches, and join the bodice shoulder seams. Press. Repeat with the lining.

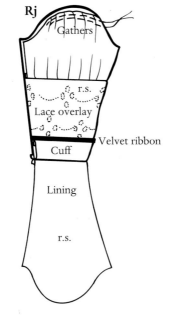

Rj

Gathers

r.s.

Lace overlay

Velvet ribbon

Cuff

Lining

r.s.

4 Tack the lace overlay to the lower sleeve on the shaded area of the pattern.

5 Gather the heading and bottom edge of the puff sleeve.

6 (Rh) With r.s.f., sew the puff sleeve to the main sleeve along the placement line. Turn the puff sleeve upwards so that the w.s. of the puff lies against the r.s. of the main sleeve. Tack the heading of the puff to the heading of the main sleeve and gather up to fit the armhole.

7 (Ri) R.s.f., sew the cuff to the sleeve along the placement line, and press downwards. Sew velvet ribbon to the top of the cuff.

8 (Rj) R.s.f., sew sleeve lining to sleeve at wrist edge.

9 Repeat Instructions 4-8 with the other sleeve.

10 R.s.f., sew sleeves to the armholes.

11 (Rk) With r.s.f., and matching armhole seams, sew up the bodice side seams, and down sleeve seams, across wrist edges and along sleeve linings.

12 Sew up bodice lining side seams.

13 With r.s.f., sew the bodice to bodice lining up the back opening, around the neck and down the other side. Clip seams, turn to the right side and press.

14 Push sleeve linings to the inside. Turn under a narrow hem around the armhole edge on each sleeve lining and hand sew to the bodice lining.

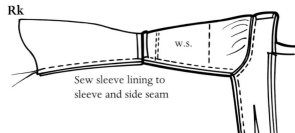

Rk

w.s.

Sew sleeve lining to sleeve and side seam

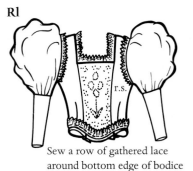

Rl

r.s.

Sew a row of gathered lace around bottom edge of bodice

15 Gather a length of narrow lace and hand stitch around the neckline and armholes.

16 (Rl) Sew a row of gathered lace around the bottom edge of the bodice taking care not to catch the lining.

17 Turn a small hem to the inside on the bodice and bodice lining, hand stitch together enclosing the raw edges.

18 Position five hooks and eyes equally down the back opening and stitch in place. Sew a jet bead above each hook.

19 (Rm) Optional: decorate the front lace panel with small beads and sequins, and scatter a few beads on the sleeve lace overlay.

Evening bag★

The bag is lined and has a chain handle; it fastens with a bead and a stitched loop. The decorative clasp in the photograph (page 29) is half a buckle.

Materials and notions

10cm (4in) cotton velvet 20cm (8in) wide

10cm (4in) silk 20cm (8in) wide for the lining – there is sufficient fabric in the measurement given for the bodice (opposite)

One bead, the size of an orange pip

40cm (12in) chain or cord

Half a decorative buckle

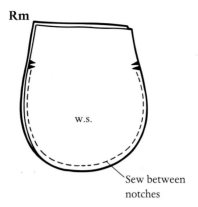

Rm

w.s.

Sew between notches

Pattern pieces There is one pattern piece for the evening bag, numbered R20.

Making instructions

1 (Rm) R.s.f., seam the front and back of the bag together down the sides and round the bottom of the bag between the notches.
2 Repeat with the lining.
3 With the lining tucked inside the bag, r.s. of lining to r.s. of bag, sew the lining to the bag from the notches up the sides and around the top leaving an opening for turning.
4 Clip seams and turn to the right side. Close the opening with hand stitching.
5 (Rn) Make two small pleats on each side of the top and stitch in place.
6 Hand stitch the chain (or cord) around the seam line leaving a loop for the handle.
7 (Ro) Sew the buckle to the front of the bag.
8 To fasten the bag make a thread loop on one side of the top and sew the bead to the other.

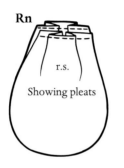

Rn

r.s.

Showing pleats

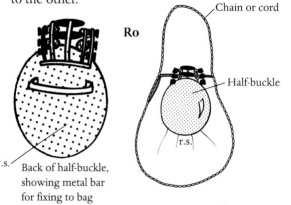

Ro

Chain or cord

Half-buckle

r.s.

w.s.

Back of half-buckle, showing metal bar for fixing to bag

Petticoat★

The back-fastening petticoat is made of fine silk. It has an overlay of antique lace which is ruched at the front and decorated with small flowers.

Materials and notions

30cm (12in) silk 80cm (31½in) wide
80cm (31½in) antique lace 20cm (8in) deep
Six small flowers
80cm (31½in) narrow lace
50cm (20in) narrow ribbon
Sewing thread to match

Pattern pieces There are two pattern pieces for the petticoat, numbered R13 and R14.

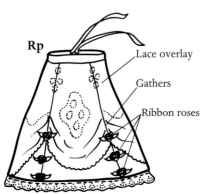

Rp

Lace overlay

Gathers

Ribbon roses

Making instructions

1 Using a French seam, sew the front to the side back; repeat with the other side back. Seam up the centre back seam, remembering to leave a small opening at the waist edge. Press.
2 Turn up a small hem at the bottom of the skirt and stitch in place. Sew a row of narrow lace around the hem.
3 With r.s.f., sew the seams on the lace overlay. Trim close to the seam.
4 Place the w.s. of the overlay over the r.s. of the petticoat and, with raw edges level, gather the waist edge. Pull up the gathers keeping most of the fullness towards the back.

5 R.s.f., stitch the waistband in place, turn to the w.s., turn under a small hem and hand stitch in place leaving the ends open.
6 Hand stitch around the back opening. Thread narrow ribbon through the waistband.
7 (Rp) Gather the lace down the seam line on either side of the front panel, pull up and attach roses at the top of the gathers. Sew roses beneath the gathers.

Cage crinoline⋆

The cage crinoline became popular from 1856 onwards. It liberated fashionable ladies from the huge weight of petticoats previously worn, between six and ten at a time. Crinolines reached such large proportions that they made life difficult for the wearer – even passing through a doorway was hazardous. So adaptations were made.

Some crinolines were hinged, and others could be pulled up by means of a cord (like venetian blinds!). Modesty often went with the wind. The crinoline was so light that it tilted easily and revealed the wearer's undergarments. The cage crinoline became a source of ridicule in cartoons of the period.

The popularity of the crinoline lasted until around 1867 when skirts became flatter at the front with the fullness towards the back.

Materials and notions
3.10m (122in) narrow boning or wire
3.10m (122in) tape 2.5cm (1in) wide
2.20m (87in) tape 1.5cm (½in) wide
90cm (35½in) narrow lace 1cm (⅜in) wide
Six small bows
85cm (33½in) flowered braid

Pattern pieces None.

Making instructions
1 (Rq) Cut a 90cm (35½in) length of 2.5cm (1in) wide tape, fold in half lengthways and sew together to make a tube.
2 Insert a 90cm (35½in) length of boning into the tube, overlap the ends and close the tape edges to form a continuous circle.
3 Repeat Instructions 1-2 using a 85cm (33½in) length of tape and boning.
4 Repeat Instructions 1-2 using a 75cm (29½in) length of tape and boning.
5 Repeat Instructions 1-2 using a 60cm (24in) length of tape and boning.
6 Cut six narrow tapes 20 cm (8in) long and position them evenly around the largest hoop. Stitch in place.
7 Attach the 85cm (33½in) hoop to the tapes 4cm (1½in) above the bottom hoop, attach the 75cm (29½in) hoop to the tapes 4cm (1½in) above the second hoop and the 60cm (24in) hoop 4cm (1½in) above this.
8 Stitch the tops of the six narrow tapes to the remaining 30cm (12in) of tape at 1cm (½in) intervals (three on each side of the centre) leaving the two ends free to tie round the doll's waist.
9 (Rr) Sew a length of lace to the bottom hoop.
10 Sew a bow where each vertical tape meets the bottom hoop.
11 Sew the flowered braid round the next hoop up from the bottom.

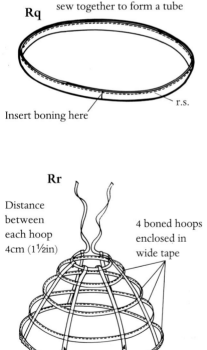

Rq
Fold tape in half lengthways and sew together to form a tube
r.s.
Insert boning here

Rr
Distance between each hoop 4cm (1½in)
4 boned hoops enclosed in wide tape
Narrow tape

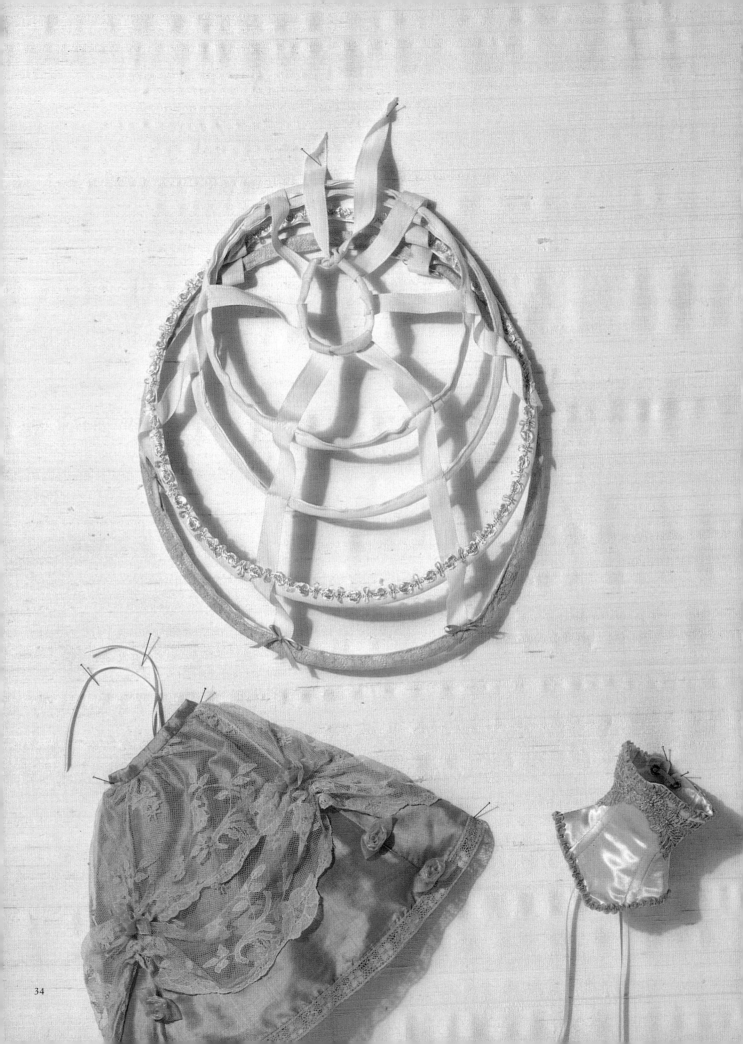

Rs

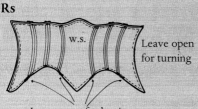

w.s.

Leave open for turning

Leave open for boning

Rt

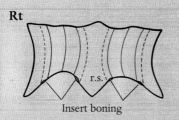

r.s.

Insert boning

Ru

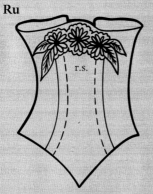

r.s.

Front showing position of motif

Rv

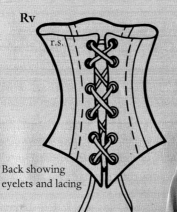

r.s.

Back showing eyelets and lacing

Corset ★

The boned corset is self lined and back fastening. As the corset needs to be a snug fit, check your doll's measurements and adjust the pattern if necessary.

Materials and notions

15cm (6in) fairly stiff satin 80cm (32in) wide
35cm (13½in) boning 0.5cm (¼in) wide – if necessary, cut wider boning in half, or use thin wire
One lace motif
Small beads
Twelve eyelets, or six hooks and eyes – if you are using eyelets you will need a length of very narrow ribbon or tape 70cm (27½in) long
Sewing thread to match
1.2m (47in) ribbon 2mm (⅛in) wide for the ribbon braid

Pattern pieces There are three pattern pieces for the corset, numbered R15 to R17.

Making instructions

1 With r.s.f., seam the corset front to the corset side pieces.
2 R.s.f., sew a back to a side back, repeat with the other two back sections.
3 R.s.f., sew the side seams together, clip and press all seams.
4 Repeat Instructions 1-3 with the lining.
5 (Rs) With r.s.f., sew the lining to the corset around the edge, leaving openings along the bottom to thread the bones through and an opening in the back for turning.
6 Clip seams and turn to the r.s., press.
7 (Rt) Sew boning channels as indicated and insert boning.
8 Hand sew the channels closed along the bottom edge.
9 (Ru) Hand stitch the decorative motif to the front and trim with a few small beads.
10 (Rv) Sew hooks and eyes or use eyelets and tape to fasten the back.
11 Make ruched ribbon braid as follows (page 36) and hand sew to the top and bottom edges of the corset.

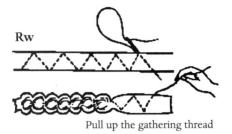

Rw

Rw

Pull up the gathering thread

Ruched ribbon braid

1 (Rw) Using a single thread and a short running stitch, hand stitch zigzags across the ribbon.
2 (Rw) Pull up the thread every few inches.
3 Continue along the length of ribbon, stitching and then pulling up the thread.
4 Attach the braid to the garment by hand stitching along the centre of the braid.

Split leg combinations ★

The lace-trimmed combinations are half-lined and have a drawstring at the top, waist and legs.

Materials and notions

25cm (10in) very soft satin 80cm (32in) wide
1.40m (55in) lace 1cm (⅜in) wide
35cm (14in) lace 2cm (1in) wide
1.40m (55in) ribbon 2mm (⅛in) wide
30cm (12in) ribbon 1cm (⅜in) wide for the straps
Two small motifs

Pattern pieces There are two pattern pieces for the split leg combinations, numbered R18 and R19.

Making instructions

1 Neaten all edges.
2 R.s.f., stitch the centre back seam, press.
3 (Rx) Sew a strip of narrow lace to each ribbon shoulder strap.
4 Pin the shoulder straps in place.
5 (Ry) With r.s.f. and raw edges level sew the half-lining to the combinations along the top, at the same time sewing the shoulder straps in place. Turn to the r.s. and press.
6 (Rz) With r.s.f., sew up the front body seam from the notch up towards the top, leaving a small opening for the drawstring at the waist and top edge; continue down the half-lining. Press.
7 Sew a row of narrow lace on the r.s. around the top edge of the combinations.
8 (Raa) Sew a row of stitching 0.5cm (¼in) from the bottom edge of the lace. This makes the casing for the top ribbon.

Rx

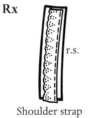

r.s.

Shoulder strap

Ry

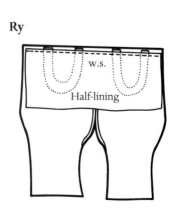

w.s.

Half-lining

Rz

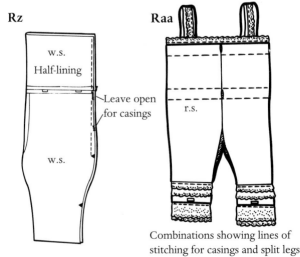

Raa

Rbb

Motifs

Combinations showing lines of stitching for casings and split legs

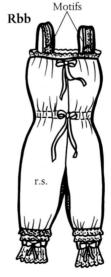

9 (Raa) Sew two rows of stitching around the waist for the drawstring.

10 Make the buttonholes on the leg fronts.

11 Sew two rows of narrow lace to the legs on the lace placement lines.

12 R.s.f., sew the leg seams from the notch downwards.

13 Turn up a wide single hem around the bottom of each leg. (This hem makes the bottom casing.) Stitch a row of wide lace along the bottom of each leg.

14 Thread 2mm (⅛in) wide ribbon through the casings around the top, waist and legs.

15 (Rbb) Hand sew small motifs to the front.

Shoes *

The shoes tie at the ankle with ribbon and have a decoration on the front. Renée has very small feet, so do check that the shoes will fit your doll. Stand your doll on a piece of paper and draw round your doll's foot. Cut out the shape and compare the cut-out with the pattern of the sole. Adjust the shoe pattern where necessary.

Materials and notions

10cm (4in) thin soft leather 15cm (6in) wide
6cm (2½in) thick leather for the soles
Thick cardboard for the insoles, picture mounting quality
Thin card for the sole infills
Glue (contact adhesive)
50cm (20in) ribbon 2mm (⅛in) wide
Two small motifs for decorating the fronts
A craft knife is useful for cutting the slits for the ribbon

Rcc

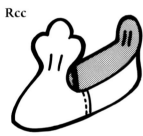

Stitch seams

Rdd

Stick motif to shoe and thread ribbon through slits

Pattern pieces There are five pattern pieces for the shoes, numbered R20 to R24.

Making instructions

1 Cut the slits in the front and back of the shoes as marked on the pattern.

2 Stick the shoe front to shoe back at A, w.s. of shoe front overlapping r.s. of shoe back.

3 (Rcc) Stitch the seams. If the leather does not travel under the machine smoothly, place a piece of paper under the seam.

4 Put a layer of glue around the shaded area of the cardboard sole.

5 Using the doll's foot as a last, put the shoe on the foot, place the cardboard sole on the bottom of the foot (glue side facing outwards). Pull the bottom of the shoe downwards and bend smoothly over the cardboard sole so that the leather sticks to the sole.

6 Remove the shoe from the foot, stick the infill on to the cardboard sole in the gap between the leather.

7 Stick the leather sole to the shoe.

8 Stick the leather heel in place.

9 Sew or stick the motif to the shoe front.

10 (Rdd) Thread ribbon through the slits in the shoe so that the tie is at the front.

11 Repeat with the second shoe.

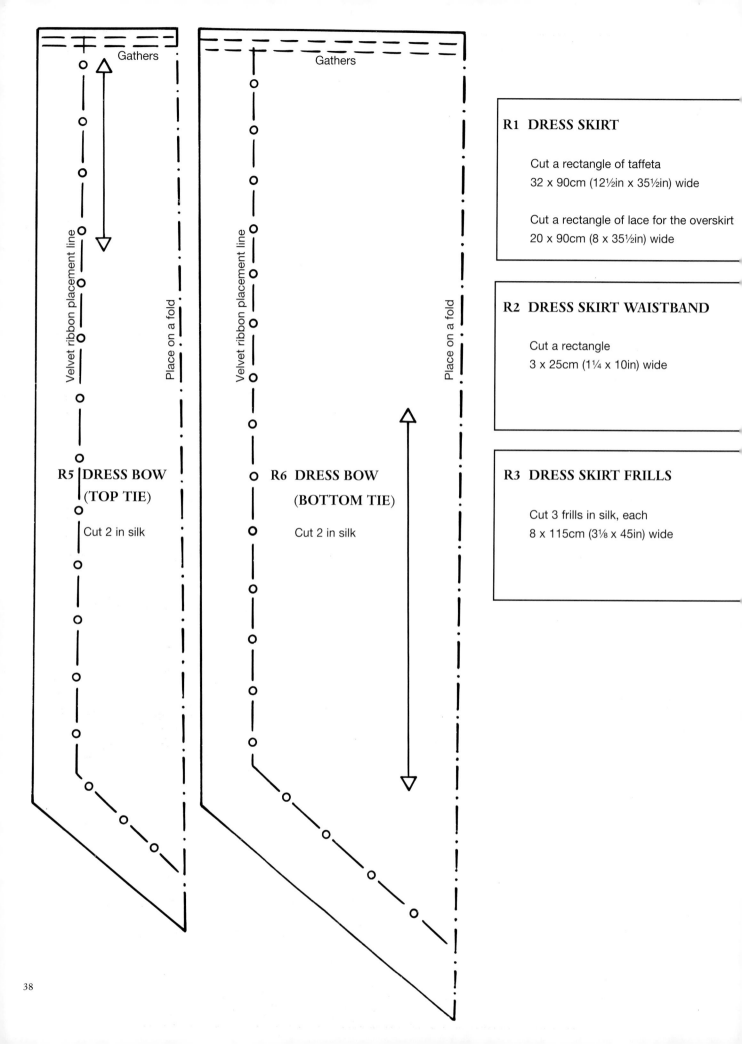

Gathers

Velvet ribbon placement line

Place on a fold

Gathers

Velvet ribbon placement line

Place on a fold

R5 DRESS BOW (TOP TIE)

Cut 2 in silk

R6 DRESS BOW (BOTTOM TIE)

Cut 2 in silk

R1 DRESS SKIRT

Cut a rectangle of taffeta
32 x 90cm (12½in x 35½in) wide

Cut a rectangle of lace for the overskirt
20 x 90cm (8 x 35½in) wide

R2 DRESS SKIRT WAISTBAND

Cut a rectangle
3 x 25cm (1¼ x 10in) wide

R3 DRESS SKIRT FRILLS

Cut 3 frills in silk, each
8 x 115cm (3⅛ x 45in) wide

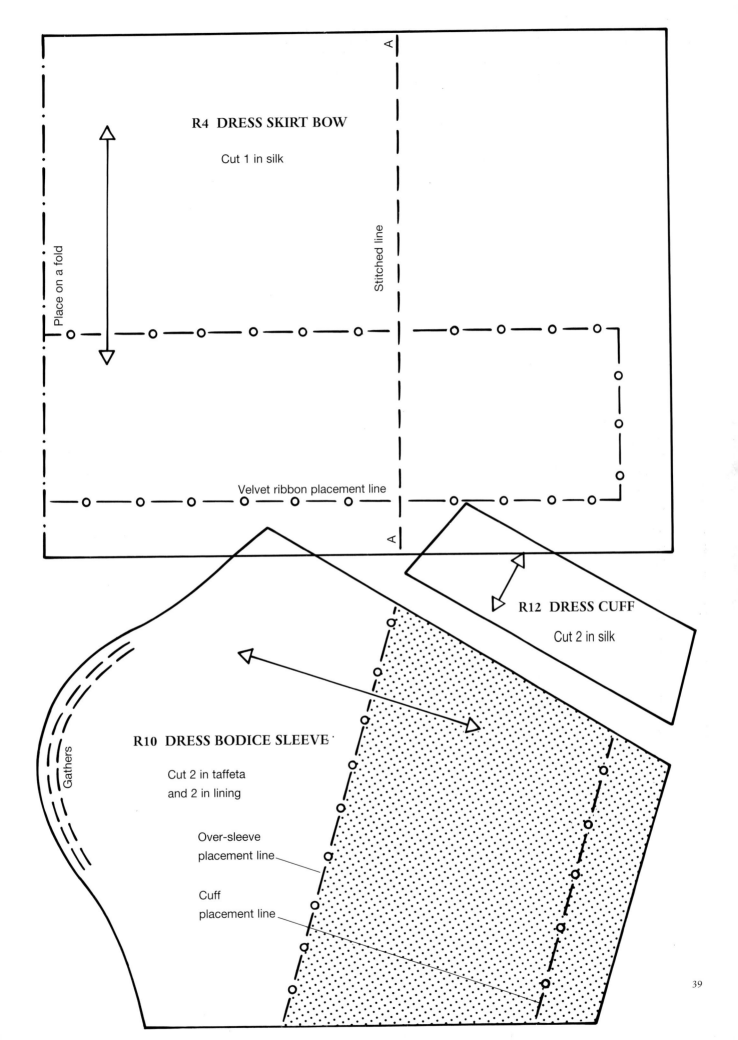

R4 DRESS SKIRT BOW

Cut 1 in silk

Place on a fold

Stitched line

A

A

Velvet ribbon placement line

R12 DRESS CUFF

Cut 2 in silk

R10 DRESS BODICE SLEEVE

Cut 2 in taffeta
and 2 in lining

Gathers

Over-sleeve
placement line

Cuff
placement line

39

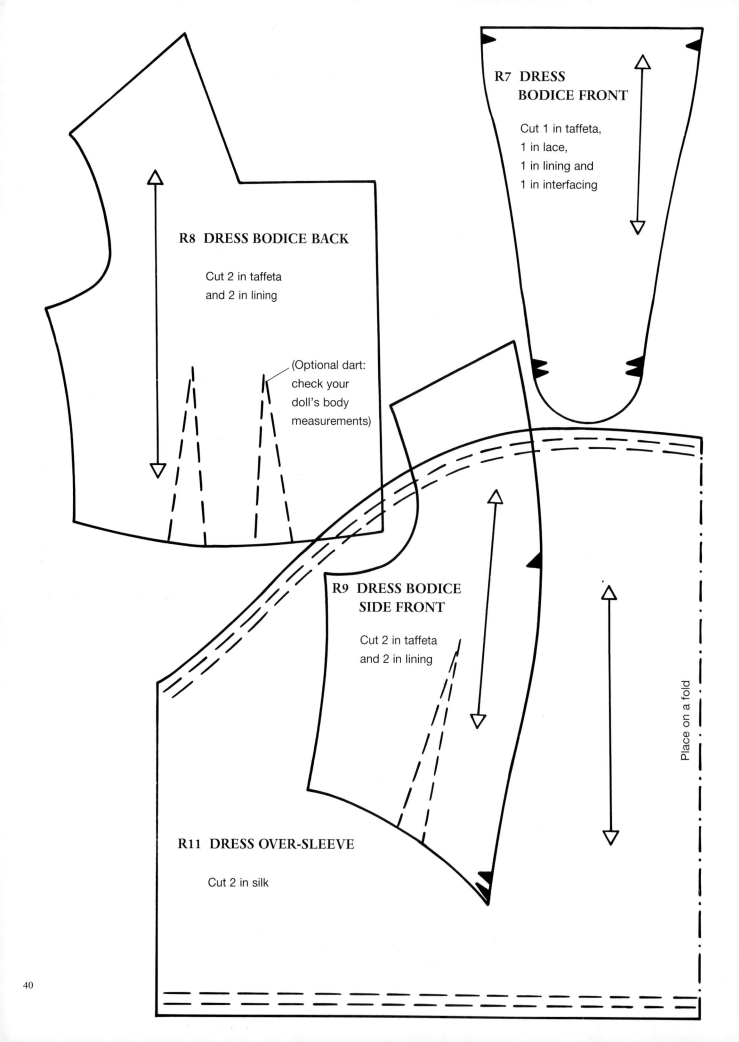

**R7 DRESS
BODICE FRONT**

Cut 1 in taffeta,
1 in lace,
1 in lining and
1 in interfacing

R8 DRESS BODICE BACK

Cut 2 in taffeta
and 2 in lining

(Optional dart:
check your
doll's body
measurements)

**R9 DRESS BODICE
SIDE FRONT**

Cut 2 in taffeta
and 2 in lining

R11 DRESS OVER-SLEEVE

Cut 2 in silk

Place on a fold

40

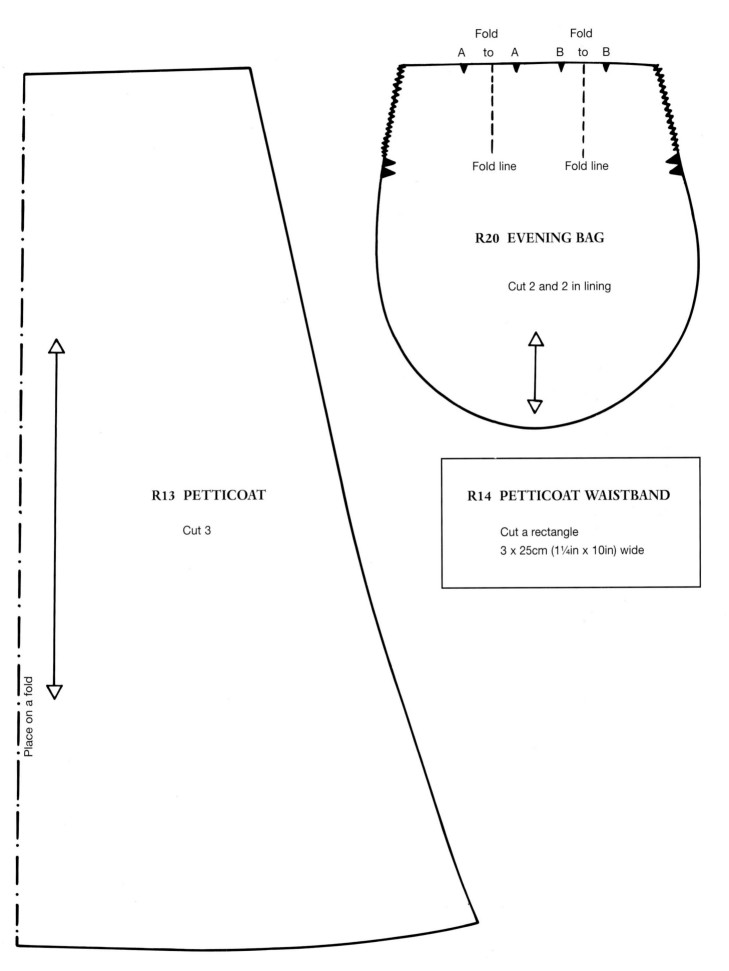

Fold A to A

Fold B to B

Fold line

Fold line

R20 EVENING BAG

Cut 2 and 2 in lining

R14 PETTICOAT WAISTBAND

Cut a rectangle
3 x 25cm (1¼in x 10in) wide

R13 PETTICOAT

Cut 3

Place on a fold

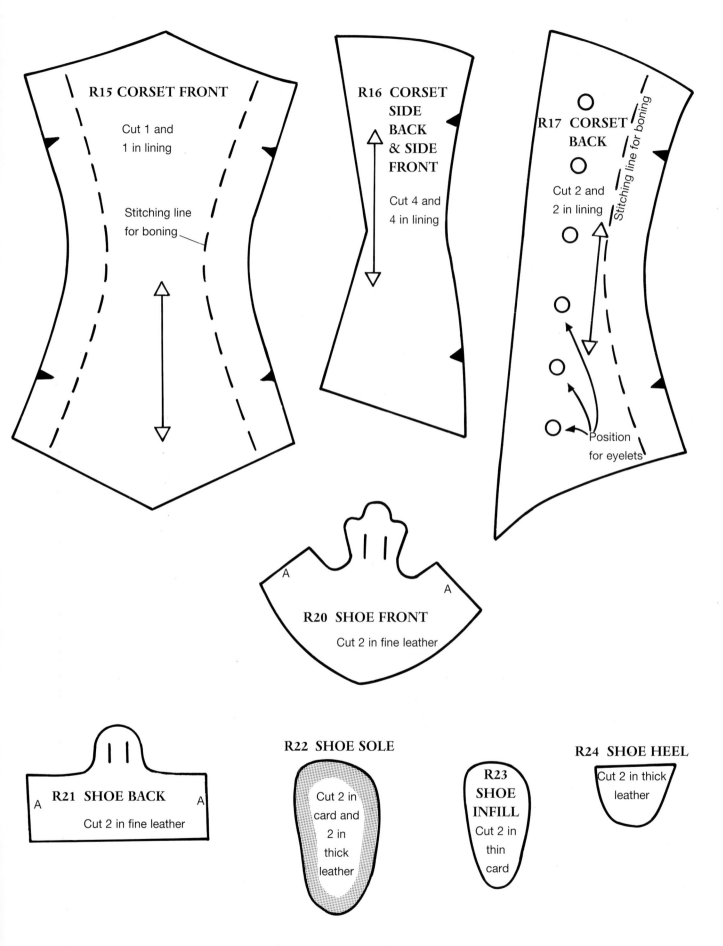

R15 CORSET FRONT

Cut 1 and
1 in lining

Stitching line
for boning

R16 CORSET SIDE BACK & SIDE FRONT

Cut 4 and
4 in lining

R17 CORSET BACK

Stitching line for boning

Cut 2 and
2 in lining

Position
for eyelets

R20 SHOE FRONT

Cut 2 in fine leather

R21 SHOE BACK

Cut 2 in fine leather

R22 SHOE SOLE

Cut 2 in
card and
2 in
thick
leather

R23 SHOE INFILL

Cut 2 in
thin
card

R24 SHOE HEEL

Cut 2 in thick
leather

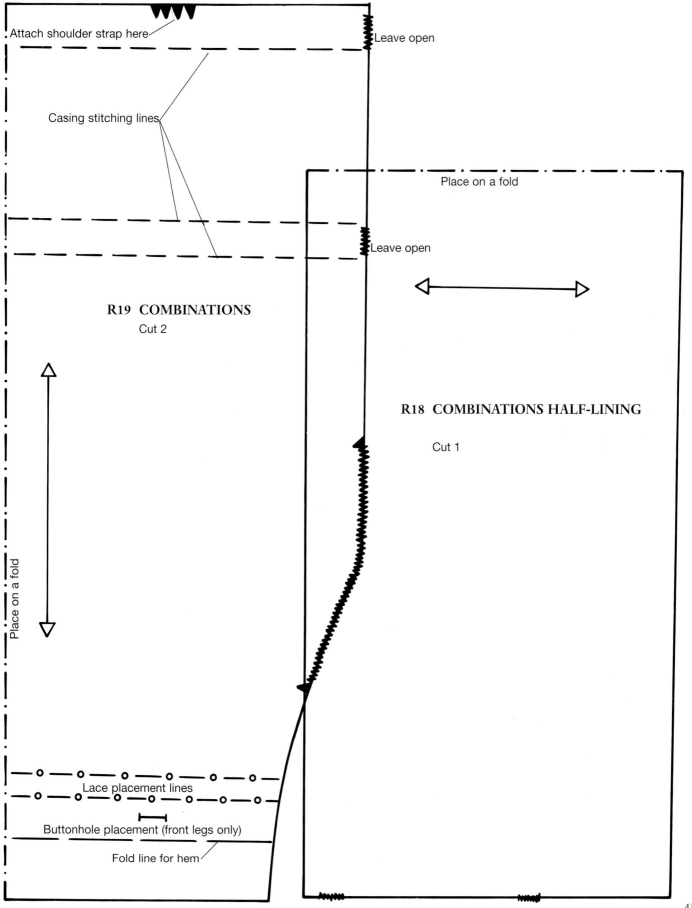

Attach shoulder strap here

Leave open

Casing stitching lines

Place on a fold

Leave open

R19 COMBINATIONS
Cut 2

Place on a fold

R18 COMBINATIONS HALF-LINING

Cut 1

Lace placement lines

Buttonhole placement (front legs only)

Fold line for hem

VERONICA

Romantic silk and satin ensemble

Veronica's striking dress and bonnet reflect the romantic Victorian period when dresses were made of luxury fabrics adorned with ribbons, laces, frills and flounces. Her dress is swathed with fine silk satin and decorated with bows, gathered lace, pin tucks and ribbon ruffles. She carries a lace parasol to protect her face from the sun. This doll is a reproduction of a French doll produced by the Bru factory. She has well-moulded features and is marked 'Bru Jne 8'. Her porcelain head has glass paperweight eyes and her body is composition. She has pierced ears and her wig is of mohair which has been curled on drinking straws. Veronica's outfit consists of dress, hat, petticoat, split leg combinations, socks, shoes and open parasol.

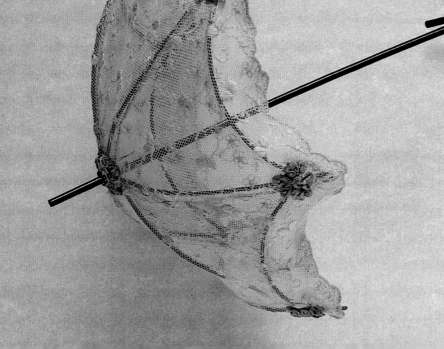

Dimensions

Height: 40cm (16in)

Circumference of head: 25cm (10in)

Neck: 16.5cm (6½in)

Waist: 23cm (9in)

Dress★★

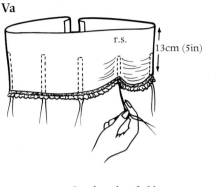

Va

13cm (5in)

r.s.

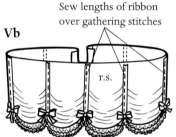

Vb

Sew lengths of ribbon
over gathering stitches

r.s.

Hand sew bows to bottom of ribbon

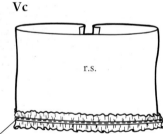

Vc

r.s.

Sew a length of velvet ribbon
along centre of gathered ribbon

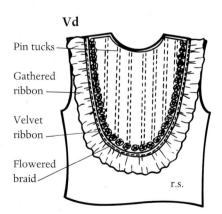

Vd

Pin tucks

Gathered
ribbon

Velvet
ribbon

Flowered
braid

r.s.

Pattern pieces There are 23 pattern pieces for Veronica's entire outfit, numbered V1 to V23 and printed on pages 54-57.

The dress is ornate and lavishly trimmed. It has a satin skirt with a gathered taffeta ribbon frill at the hem. The lace-edged, swathed silk overskirt is profusely decorated with ribbon, lace and bows. The bodice is pin-tucked and frilled. The lace is coloured to match the fabric using fabric paints.

Materials and notions

37cm (14½in) stiff violet satin 115cm (45in) wide
52cm (20½in) lilac silk satin 115cm (45in) wide, for the overskirt and lining
2m (78½in) taffeta ribbon 6cm (2½in) wide
2m (78½in) satin ribbon 1cm (⅜in) wide
2.30m (91in) velvet ribbon 0.5cm (¼in) wide
1m (39in) velvet ribbon 3cm (1¼in) wide for the sash
2.30cm (91in) lace 1cm (⅜in) wide
1m (39in) flowered braid
Six hooks and eyes
Four buttons
Beads
Decorative buckle for the sash (optional)
Sewing threads to match

Pattern pieces There are nine pattern pieces for the dress, numbered V1 to V9. Do not cut out V3 until Instruction 13.

Making instructions

1 R.s.f., sew up the back seam of the skirt leaving a 5cm (2in) opening at the waist edge. Neaten the seam and press.
2 Press up and stitch a narrow double hem around the bottom edge of the skirt.
3 Repeat Instructions 1-2 with the overskirt.
4 Sew a row of gathered lace on the r.s. around the hem of the overskirt.
5 Sew a row of flat lace just overlapping the gathered lace.
6 Divide the overskirt into eight equal sections and mark with pins on the hem.
7 Run two rows of gathering threads from each pin towards the waist stopping 5cm (2in) from the waist edge.
8 (Va) Pull up the gathers so the skirt measures 13cm (5in). Sew a length of satin ribbon from the waist to the hem covering the gathering stitches. Hand sew a ribbon bow to the bottom of the ribbon (Vb). Repeat with all eight sections.
9 Cut a 1.70m length of taffeta ribbon and stitch a row of gathering stitches down the centre. Pull up to fit round the bottom of the skirt.
10 (Vc) Sew the ribbon to the r.s. of the skirt around the hem, sewing along the row of gathering stitches. Sew a row of narrow velvet ribbon along the centre of the taffeta ribbon.
11 Put the w.s. of the overskirt over the r.s. of the skirt, and with raw edges level stitch two rows of gathering threads around the waist.
12 Using a double needle make rows of pin tucks down the front bib rectangle.
13 Cut out the bib shape (V3) and sew to the r.s. of the bodice front.
14 Cut the remainder of the taffeta ribbon in half lengthways and using one half gather it along the raw edge.
15 (Vd) Stitch the gathered ribbon around the edge of the bib shape, sewing on top of the gathering stitches.

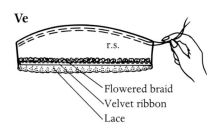

Ve

r.s.

Flowered braid
Velvet ribbon
Lace

16 (Vd) Sew a length of narrow velvet ribbon to cover the raw edge of the taffeta ribbon – hand sewing is easier.

17 (Vd) Sew a length of flowered braid inside the velvet ribbon.

18 R.s.f., sew the shoulder seams. Press.

19 Press a narrow single hem to the r.s of the cap sleeve along the straight edge. Sew a row of flat lace along the hem. Sew a length of narrow velvet ribbon just touching the lace and then a row of flowered braid inside the ribbon.

20 (Ve) Gather the curved edge of the cap sleeve and, with r.s.f., sew round the dress armhole.

21 Using a double needle make pin tucks on the bottom half of the sleeve rectangle. Lay the sleeve pattern on the pin tucks and cut to shape.

22 Gather the sleeve heading to fit the armhole and sew the sleeve in place. Repeat Instructions 19-22 with the second sleeve.

23 R.s.f., sew along sleeve seam across armhole and down the side seam. Repeat with the other side.

24 R.s.f., sew the lining shoulder seams, press.

25 Gather the lining sleeve headings and, with r.s.f., sew to the lining armholes.

26 With r.s.f., sew along the sleeve seam and down the side seam of the lining. Repeat and press.

27 R.s.f., sew bodice to bodice lining up the back edge, around the neck and down the other back opening. Clip seams, turn to the r.s. and press.

28 Pull up the gathers on the skirt to fit the bodice leaving a small overlap for fastening. With r.s.f., sew skirt to bodice taking care not to catch the bodice lining in the seam.

29 Turn a small hem to the inside on the bodice lining and hand stitch around the waist.

30 Turn a hem to the w.s. at the bottom of the sleeve and sleeve lining. Hand stitch together enclosing the raw edges. The lining will be shorter than the sleeve; this makes the top of the sleeve puff up. Repeat with the other sleeve.

31 Hand stitch a row of narrow velvet ribbon round the wrist edge of the sleeves.

32 Sew four hooks and eyes to the bodice back. Sew small buttons on top of the hooks for decoration.

33 Hand stitch a length of narrow velvet ribbon around the neck edge.

34 Sew beads to the centres of the flowers on the flowered braid and sew a cluster of beads just above each bow on the overskirt.

35 Put the wide velvet ribbon sash around your doll's waist and tie a bow at the back. Alternatively, slot the cut edges through a decorative buckle.

Hat★

Large, frivolous hats were a popular fashion feature of this era. Veronica's hat is ruched on wires and is a profusion of lace, ribbon and flowers.

Materials and notions
23cm (9in) violet satin 85cm (33½in) wide
23cm (9in) lilac silk satin 85cm (33½in) wide for the lining
Millinery wire, one of each of the following lengths: 20cm (8in), 28cm (11in), 32cm (12½in), 35cm (14in)
50cm (19½in) lace 8cm (3in) wide
25cm (10in) narrow lace (for dyeing, see page 9)
40cm (16in) taffeta ribbon – there is sufficient in the half width left from the bodice bib (page 46)
1.80m (71in) transparent ribbon 4cm (1½in) wide
Seven flowers

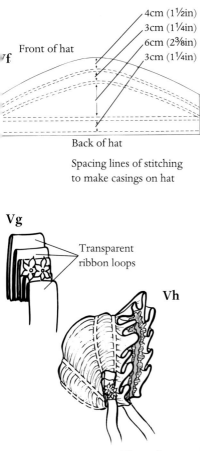

4cm (1½in)
3cm (1¼in)
6cm (2⅜in)
3cm (1¼in)

Front of hat

Vf

Back of hat

Spacing lines of stitching
to make casings on hat

Vg

Transparent
ribbon loops

Vh

Pattern pieces There are two pattern pieces for the hat, numbered V10 and V11.

Making instructions

1 R.s.f., and raw edges level, sew the lining to the hat around the edge leaving one of the narrow side edges open. Turn and press a narrow hem to the inside of the lining of the hat, along the open edge.
2 (Vf) Sew two rows of stitching to form a casing 1cm (⅜in) apart on the four lines indicated across the hat.
3 Bend a loop in one end of each wire.
4 Thread the wires (loops first) through the casings, rouching the hat as you go. The shortest wire is inserted at the neck edge (the casing right on the edge of the fabric), then the next shortest and so on. Pin the loops to the edge of the hat.
5 Bend the hat and adjust wires to fit your doll's head.
6 Make loops at the other end of the wires and hand sew the loops to the hat, close the side opening.
7 Fold over one-third of the wide lace lengthways and gather on the folded edge. Pull up to fit the casing at the front of the head.
8 Gather the ribbon along the cut edge and sew to the gathered edge of the lace.
9 Place the gathered frill along the front casing inside the hat and hand sew in place. Turning the hat inside out makes this easier. Cover the gathered edge with a row of flat lace.
10 Sew three flowers in the centre of the gathered frill.
11 (Vg; Vh) Make several loops in the transparent ribbon and sew to the sides of the hat, leaving the long ends free for the ties. Sew two flowers to each group of loops.

Petticoat★

The petticoat skirt has a front panel of tucks and lace and the lined bodice has lace panels and a central motif. The hem is also edged with a tuck and trimmed with lace and hand embroidery.

Materials and notions
50cm (20in) striped silky fabric 115cm (45in) wide
2.15m (85in) lace 3cm (1¼in) wide
One large motif for bodice front
Twelve small flower motifs for the skirt – the motifs in the photograph (page 47) were cut from flowered braid and dyed with fabric paint
Three hooks and eyes
50cm (20in) ribbon 5mm (¼in) wide for the bows
Sewing thread to match
Stranded embroidery thread

Pattern pieces There are four pattern pieces for the petticoat, numbered V12 to V15.

Vi

Folding sequence for front
panel of petticoat skirt

r.s.

Lace

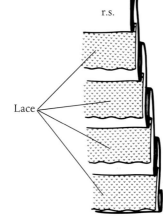

Making instructions

1 Neaten all edges.
2 Press the tucks in the front panel of the skirt and stitch the three top tucks.
3 Sew three rows or lace beneath the tucks.
4 R.s.f, sew centre back seam leaving a 5cm (2in) opening at the waist edge.
5 With r.s.f, sew front panel to skirt sides.
6 Turn up a narrow hem to the w.s and stitch in place.
7 (Vi) Press a fold 4cm (1⅝in) from the bottom of the hem to make the bottom

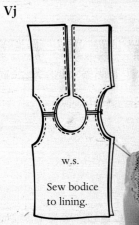

Vj

w.s.

Sew bodice
to lining.

tuck. Stitch the tuck 2cm (⅞in) from the fold. The bottom tuck on the front panel will have to be stitched separately.

8 Sew a row of lace around the hem beneath the tuck – the bottom edge of the lace is level with the bottom of the hem.

9 Run two rows of gathering stitches around the waist edge.

10 Sew two rows of lace to the bodice front as indicated on the pattern.

11 R.s.f., sew the bodice shoulder seams, press.

12 Repeat with the lining.

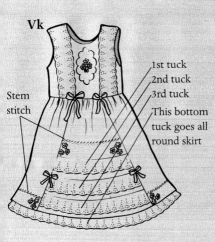

Vk

1st tuck
2nd tuck
3rd tuck

This bottom tuck goes all round skirt

Stem stitch

13 (Vj) R.s.f., sew bodice to lining up the back opening around the neck and down the other back opening. Sew round the armholes.

14 Clip seams, turn to the r.s. by pulling the backs through the shoulders. Press.

15 (Vj) R.s.f., sew up the bodice side seam, across the armhole and down the lining side seam. Repeat with the other side.

16 Pull up the gathers on the skirt to fit the bodice leaving a small overlap for fastening. With r.s.f., sew the skirt to the bodice taking care not to catch the bodice lining.

17 Turn a narrow hem to the w.s. of the bodice lining and hand stitch in place.

18 Hand stitch the motif to the bodice front.

19 Sew three hooks and eyes, evenly spaced, to the back opening.

20 Sew the flower motifs in groups of three as shown in the diagram

21 Sew two bows to the waist where the bodice lace joins the skirt and two halfway down the front panel.

22 (Vk) Hand embroider, using three strands of embroidery thread, in stem stitch as indicated.

Split leg combinations★

The lace-trimmed combinations are half-lined and have a drawstring at the neck, waist and knees.

Vl

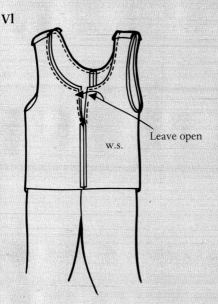

Leave open

w.s.

Materials and notions

30cm (12in) of fine soft fabric 115cm (45in) wide
1.10m (43in) narrow cotton lace
Two lace leaves for decoration – these could be motifs cut from lace.
2m (79in) satin ribbon 2mm (⅛in) wide
Sewng thread to match

Pattern pieces There are two pattern pieces for the split leg combinations, numbered V16 and V17.

Making instructions

Remember there are no side seams.

1 Neaten all edges.

2 With r.s.f., sew the centre front seam between the notches, leaving a small opening at C for the drawstring.

3 R.s.f., sew the centre back seam from the neck down to the notch and press.

4 R.s.f., sew the centre front and back seams on the half lining and press.

5 R.s.f., sew the shoulder seams, press.

6 Repeat with the half lining.

7 (Vl) R.s.f., sew the lining to combination up the front opening, around the neck and down the other front opening, leaving small gaps at A to thread the ribbon through later. Clip, turn and press.

8 From the r.s., sew a row of flat narrow lace 0.5cm (¼in) down from the neck edge. This makes the neck casing. Sew the leaf motifs to the fronts.

9 Sew a buttonhole on the leg fronts as marked.

Vm

Thread ribbon through casings

10 Sew two rows of stitching around the waist to make a casing for the draw-string. You may find it easier to keep your stitching straight if you press a crease around the waist line.

11 R.s.f., sew up leg seams from the bottom edge to the notch.

12 Turn up and stitch a 1cm (⅜in) wide single hem at the bottom of the legs. This hem will be used as a casing for the ribbon.

13 Make a length of wide lace by sewing two pieces of narrow lace together, one above the other. Sew to the r.s. around the bottom of the legs.

14 Turn a very narrow single hem to the w.s. around the crotch split and stitch in place.

15 Turn under a small hem around the armhole edge on the combinations and on the lining. With the raw edges enclosed hand stitch around the armholes.

16 (Vm) Thread narrow ribbon through the neck, waist and legs.

Socks★

Materials and notions

(To achieve the correct colour for the socks in the photograph (page 51), six-stranded embroidery cotton was used)

Four skeins of six-stranded embroidery cotton – unwind the skeins and split the threads in half. The socks are knitted with three strands of the stranded embroidery cotton

One pair 1.5mm knitting needles

Sewing up needle

Making instructions

See page 9 for abbreviations.

Cast on 42 sts, and work 7 rows of k1, p1, rib

8th row: inc 1st in the first st, rib to last st inc 1st in last st (44 sts)

Commence pattern

Row 1: K1, * yf, sl1, k2tog, psso, yf, k3, rep. from * to last st, k1

Row 2: P

Rep. rows 1 and 2 three more times

Row 9: K1, * k3, yf, sl1, k2tog, psso, yf, rep. from * to last st, k1

Row 10: P

Rep. rows 9 and 10 three more times

These 16 rows form the pattern. Rep. the 16 rows of pattern two more times (48 rows from the rib)

Foot shaping

Row 1: K30, turn

Row 2: P16

Continue on the centre 16 sts for a further 16 rows, knitting in st.st., ending with a p row

Row 19: K16, pick up and k 10 sts from along the side of the foot, continue and k the 14 sts from the left needle (40 sts)

Row 20: P40, pick up and k 10 sts purlwise from along the side of the foot, continue and p the 14 sts from the left needle (64 sts)

Heel shaping

Row 1: K2tog, k28, k2tog, k2tog, k28, k2tog

Row 2: P2tog, p26, p2tog, p2tog, p26, p2tog

Row 3: K2tog, k24, k2tog, k2tog, k24, k2tog

Row 4: P2tog, p22, p2tog, p2tog, p22, p2tog

Row 5: K2tog, k20, k2tog, k2tog, k20, k2tog
Row 6: P2tog, p18, p2tog, p2tog, p18, p2tog
Row 7: K2tog, k16, k2tog, k2tog, k16, k2tog
Cast off purlwise

Sew up foot and back seam.
Repeat for the second sock.

Shoes★

The shoes are made of fine leather. They fasten at the front with an ankle strap and are decorated with metal studs; alternatively, use small ribbon rosettes.

Materials and notions
10cm (4in) fine leather 20cm (8in) wide
10cm (4in) stiff leather 10cm (4in) wide for the soles and heels
Two decorations for the fronts – metal studs or rosettes
40cm (16in) ribbon 2cm (¾in) wide
A leather punch
Glue (contact adhesive)
Stiff cardboard, picture mounting quality
Thin card for the sole infills

Pattern pieces   There are six pattern pieces for the shoes, numbered V18 to V23.

Making instructions
1 Stick the inside side seam, shoe front overlapping shoe back, and stitch.
2 Stick and sew the other side seam.
3 Sew a row of top stitching around the inside edge of the shoe and around the straps.
4 Put a layer of glue around the outside edge of the cardboard sole (the shaded area).
5 Put the cardboard sole inside the shoe with the glue side facing outwards.
6 Pull the bottom edge of the upper down and bend it round over the glued edge of the sole, making sure the leather lies smoothly round the toe area. Hold in place while the glue dries.
7 Stick the thin card infill to the sole so that it fits neatly between the leather.
8 Stick the leather sole in place.
9 Stick the heel to the sole.
10 (Vn) Punch a hole in each strap and thread narrow ribbon through the holes.
11 Decorate the front.
12 Repeat with the other shoe.

Vn

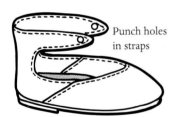

Punch holes in straps

Open parasol★

Parasol sizes vary, so here are the making instructions without measurements.
1 To make the pattern, place the top of the parasol on a piece of paper and draw round one of the triangular sections. Cut this section out adding seam allowances.
2 Using wide lace, cut out sufficient sections to cover your parasol. Dye the lace to match the outfit with fabric paint if necessary.
3 R.s.f., seam the sections together and trim away the excess seam allowance.
4 Put the lace over the top of the parasol and sew to the ends of the wire spokes.
5 Decorate with rosettes of ruched 2mm (⅛in) wide ribbon (see page 36). Hand sew one rosette at the end of each spoke and one in the centre of the top.

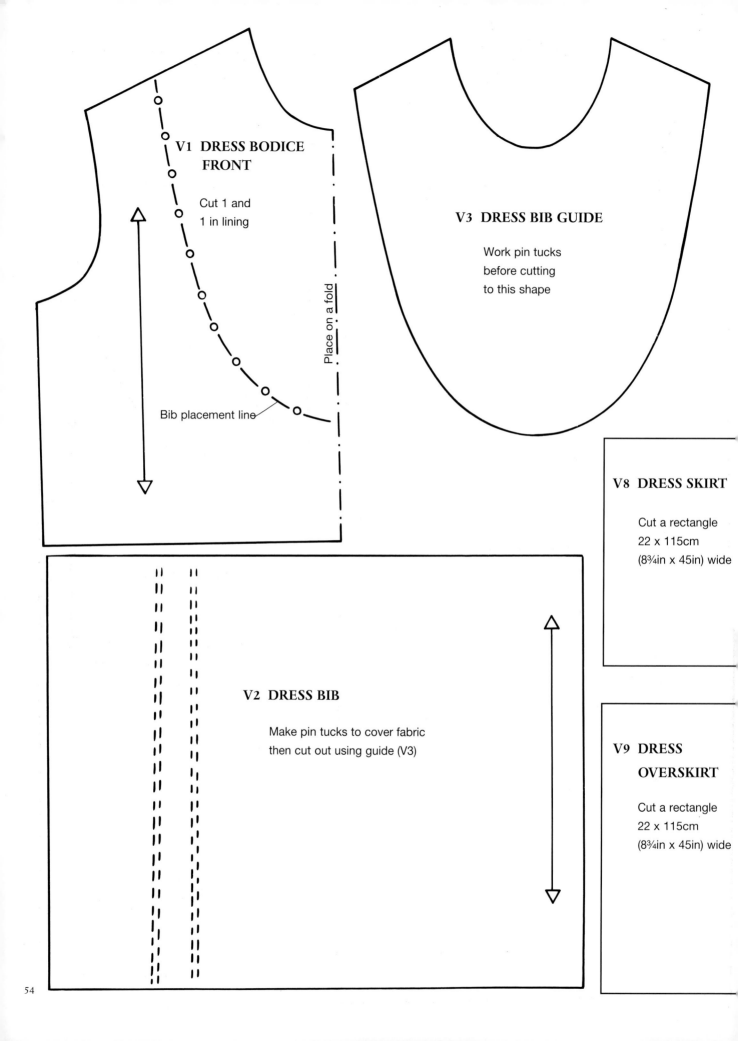

V1 DRESS BODICE FRONT

Cut 1 and
1 in lining

Place on a fold

Bib placement line

V3 DRESS BIB GUIDE

Work pin tucks
before cutting
to this shape

V8 DRESS SKIRT

Cut a rectangle
22 x 115cm
(8¾in x 45in) wide

V2 DRESS BIB

Make pin tucks to cover fabric
then cut out using guide (V3)

V9 DRESS OVERSKIRT

Cut a rectangle
22 x 115cm
(8¾in x 45in) wide

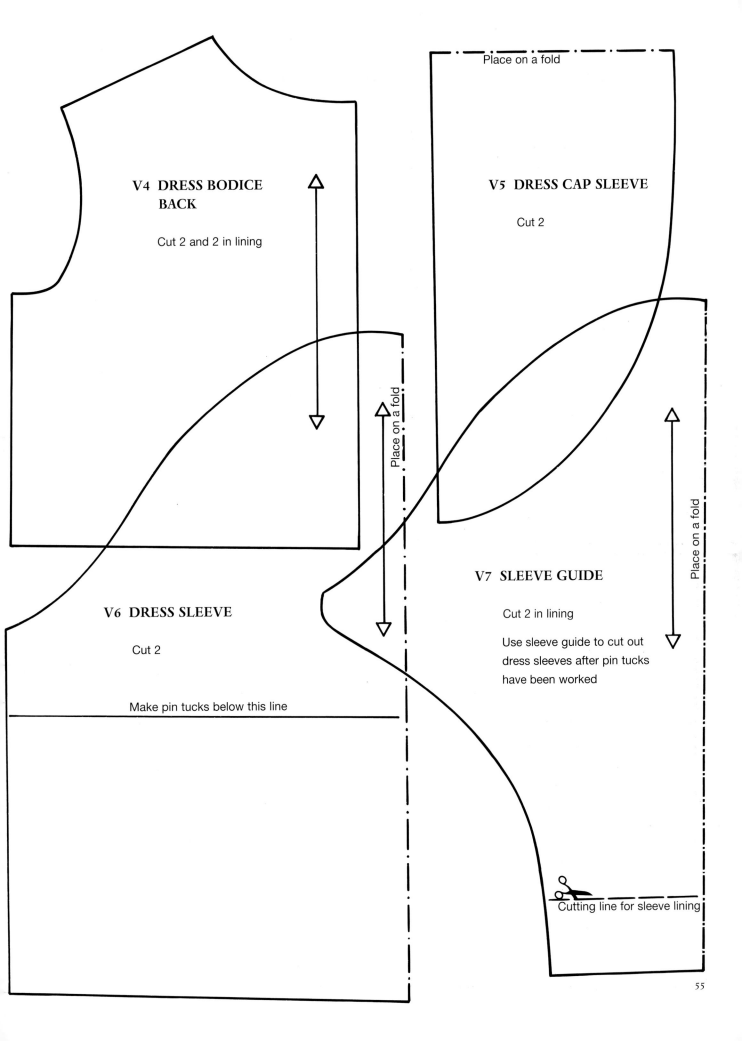

**V4 DRESS BODICE
BACK**

Cut 2 and 2 in lining

V5 DRESS CAP SLEEVE

Cut 2

Place on a fold

Place on a fold

V7 SLEEVE GUIDE

Cut 2 in lining

Use sleeve guide to cut out
dress sleeves after pin tucks
have been worked

Place on a fold

V6 DRESS SLEEVE

Cut 2

Make pin tucks below this line

Cutting line for sleeve lining

55

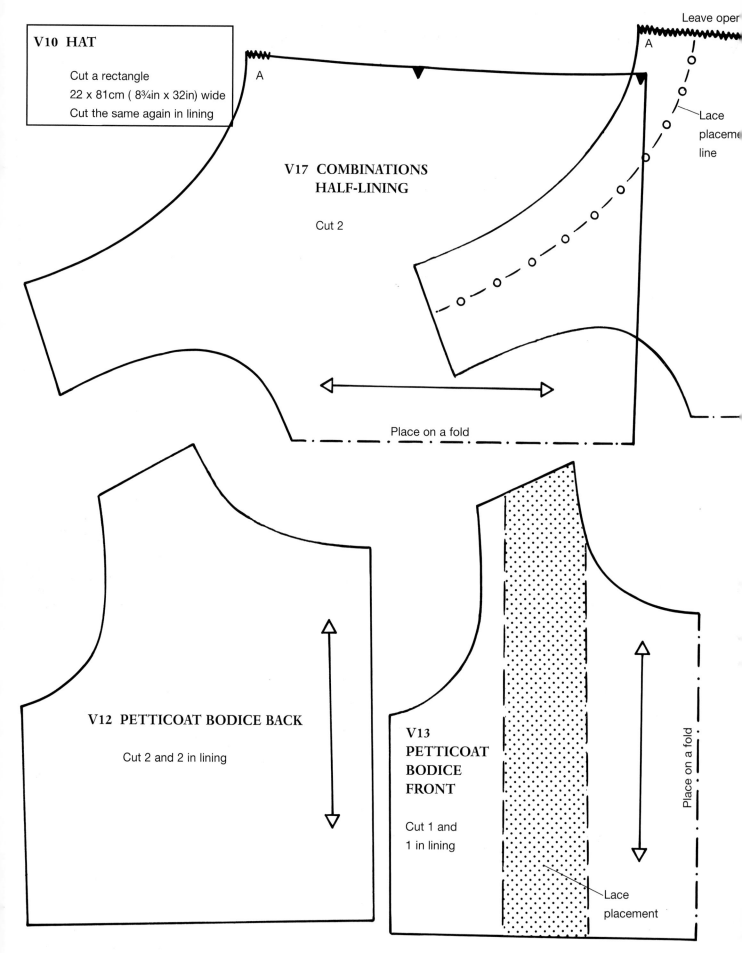

V10 HAT

Cut a rectangle
22 x 81cm (8¾in x 32in) wide
Cut the same again in lining

V17 COMBINATIONS HALF-LINING

Cut 2

A

A

Leave open

Lace placement line

Place on a fold

V12 PETTICOAT BODICE BACK

Cut 2 and 2 in lining

V13 PETTICOAT BODICE FRONT

Cut 1 and 1 in lining

Place on a fold

Lace placement

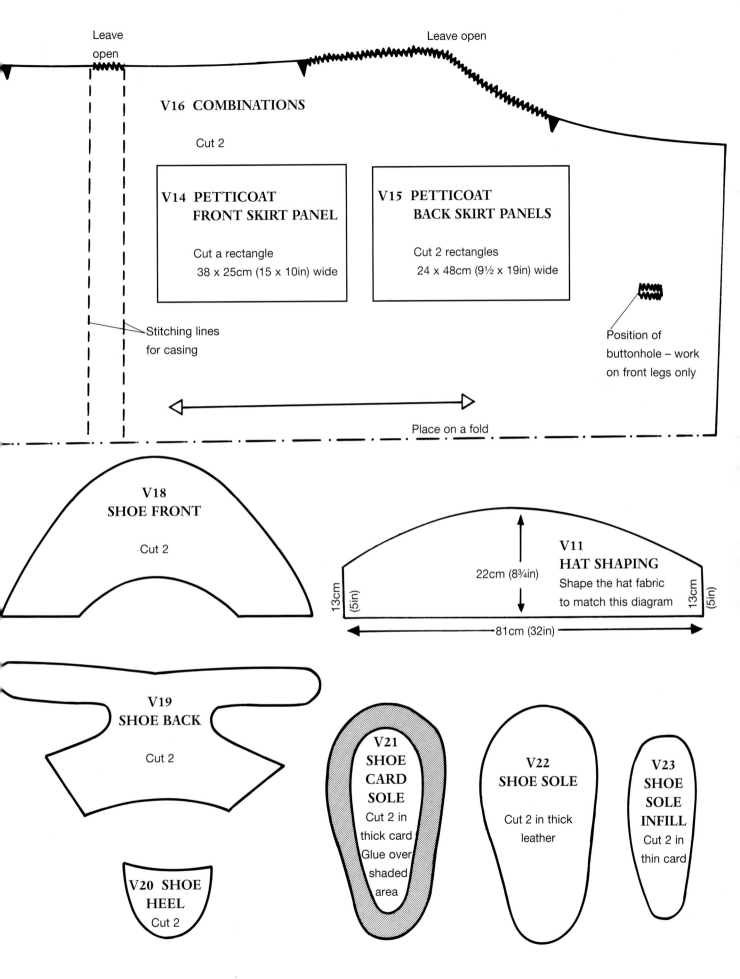

Leave open

Leave open

V16 COMBINATIONS

Cut 2

V14 PETTICOAT FRONT SKIRT PANEL

Cut a rectangle
38 x 25cm (15 x 10in) wide

V15 PETTICOAT BACK SKIRT PANELS

Cut 2 rectangles
24 x 48cm (9½ x 19in) wide

Stitching lines
for casing

Position of
buttonhole – work
on front legs only

Place on a fold

V18 SHOE FRONT

Cut 2

V11 HAT SHAPING

Shape the hat fabric
to match this diagram

22cm (8¾in)

13cm (5in)

13cm (5in)

81cm (32in)

V19 SHOE BACK

Cut 2

V21 SHOE CARD SOLE
Cut 2 in thick card
Glue over shaded area

V22 SHOE SOLE

Cut 2 in thick leather

V23 SHOE SOLE INFILL

Cut 2 in thin card

V20 SHOE HEEL
Cut 2

ANTOINETTE

Sunday best dress and coat

Antoinette's French-style outfit is typical of those worn by young girls in the latter half of the nineteenth century. The coat and dress have dropped waistlines, and the dress has a plastron and a two-tiered gathered skirt, all lavishly trimmed with ribbon, lace and braid. The doll is a reproduction of the French A. Thullier doll 'AT9'. She has a porcelain head, a composition body, glass paperweight eyes and her wig is made from mohair. Antique dolls by A. Thullier are extremely rare and command very high prices. The dolls produced by this factory are noted for their wistful expressions. Antoinette's outfit consists of coat, hat, dress, sash, petticoat, camisole, bloomers, socks and shoes.

Dimensions

Height: 43cm (17in)

Circumference of head: 25cm (10in)

Waist: 22cm (8½in)

Neck: 13cm (5¼in)

Pattern pieces There are 31 pattern pieces for Antoinette's whole outfit, numbered A1 to A31 and printed on pages 71-77.

Coat★★★

The lined coat has a cape collar and a dropped waistline. The full sleeves are narrowed by pleating at the wrist edge and the skirt has three sets of inverted pleats. A contrasting braid outlines the collar, pockets and waistline.

Materials and notions
60cm (24in) velvet 115cm (45in) wide
1m (39in) ricrac braid, dyed in tea (see page 9)
1.15m (45in) Russia braid, dyed in tea
60cm (24in) lining 115cm (45in) wide
Eleven buttons
Sewing thread to match

Aa

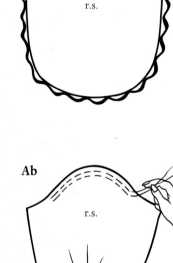

r.s.

Pattern pieces
There are eight pattern pieces for the coat, numbered A1 to A8.

Making instructions
1 Stitch ricrac braid to the r.s. of the collar and pocket flaps as indicated on the pattern. The stitching must be along the centre of the braid.
2 With r.s.f., stitch the lining to the collar sewing along the same line of stitching, leaving the neck edge open. Clip the seam, turn and press – only half of the braid will show on the r.s.
3 (Aa) Stitch the lining to the pockets in the same way.
4 R.s.f., sew the shoulder seams, press.
5 (Ab) With r.s.f., sew up the centre of the sleeve from the wrist up to the notch. Press the pleat open on the back and top stitch in place.
6 (Ab) Gather the heading of the sleeve between notches and pull up to fit armhole.
7 R.s.f., sew sleeve into armhole.
8 Repeat with second sleeve.
9 R.s.f., stitch along sleeve seam, across armhole and down side seam. Repeat with the other side.
10 Repeat from Instruction 4 with the lining but omit the top stitching.

Ab

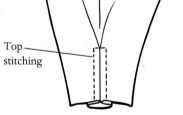

r.s.

Top stitching

11 (Ac) There are three sets of inverted pleats on the skirt of the coat: one set in the centre of the back and one set on each front below the pocket placement. Make the pleats at the top of the skirt using the pleating guide and position them as marked by the single notches on the bodice pattern. The back group of pleats has one extra pleat on each side. Run a line of stitches across the pleats to hold them in place.
12 Pin the pockets over the front pleats, raw edges level (using front bodice pattern piece for pocket placement notches). Stitch along the top of the pockets through all layers.
13 R.s.f., sew the skirt to the bodice.
14 Make a tuck around the dropped waist line, again sewing through all layers. Trim away any excess fabric from the seam.
15 Hand stitch the Russia braid to the fronts and around the waistline following the braid placement lines on the pattern.
16 Pleat the skirt lining making a large single pleat in place of the group of pleats and, with r.s.f., sew to bodice lining.
17 With r.s. of the lining against r.s. of the coat, sew down the front edges from

Ac Guide for pleating coat skirt

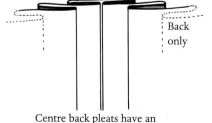

Back only

Centre back pleats have an extra pleat – follow dotted lines

Ad

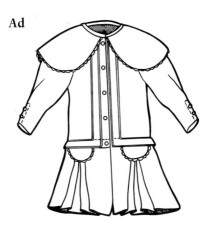

the neck to the hem, turn to the r.s. and press.

18 Run a row of stitches around the cape collar and pull up to fit between the notches on the neckline.

19 Push the sleeve linings into the sleeves, and, with w.s. of collar to r.s. of bodice, tack around the neckline through all layers.

20 R.s.f., sew the neckband in place, turn to the w.s., turn under a narrow hem and hand stitch to the lining.

21 Turn up a double hem to the w.s. of the lining, press and stitch.

22 Turn up a single hem to the w.s. of the coat and hand stitch in place.

23 Turn the raw edges of the sleeves and sleeve linings to the w.s. and hand stitch together enclosing the raw edges.

24 Position five buttons evenly down the left front.

25 Make five buttonholes on the right front to correspond with the buttons.

26 (Ad) Sew two buttons to each sleeve edge one above the other.

27 Optional: sew two buttons at the centre of the waist on the back.

Hat★

The lined crown of the hat is gathered onto a piped hatband. The front of the hat is decorated with a ribbon cocarde.

Ae

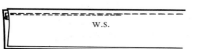

Materials and notions

Velvet – there is sufficient fabric in the amount given for the coat (page 60)

Lining – there is sufficient fabric in the amount given for the coat

35cm (14in) silky self-finished piping cord – the cord used has one flat edge which can be enclosed in the seam. Alternatively, sew a round cord on the hat by hand

1m (39in) soft petersham ribbon 4cm (1½in) wide

1.80m (71in) satin ribbon 2cm (¾in) wide

A scrap of buckram

A fancy buckle

Sewing thread to match

A hatpin

Af

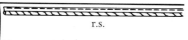

Pattern pieces There are three pattern pieces for the hat, numbered A9 to A11.

Making instructions

1 (Ae) Using the zip foot of the machine, sew the silky piping to the hatband along one long edge.

2 (Af) With r.s.f. and enclosing the cord, sew the hatband to the hatband lining, sewing on top of the previous row of stitching.

Ag

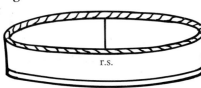

3 (Ag) Pin the back seam of the hatband to fit your doll's head and, with r.s.f., sew up the back seam. Press.

4 (Ah) W.s.f. and raw edges level, put the crown and the crown lining together. Sew two rows of gathering threads around the edge and pull up to fit the hatband.

5 With r.s.f., sew the velvet side of the hatband to the gathered crown.

6 Turn under a narrow hem on the hatband lining and hand stitch in place round the inside of the hat.

Ah

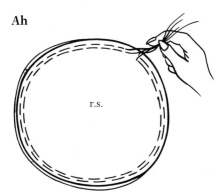

Ai

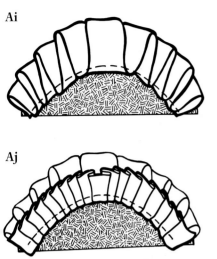

To make the ribbon cocarde

1 (Ai) Working from the diagram, sew a row of satin ribbon loops round the top of the fan-shaped buckram.
2 (Aj) Sew a row of pleated petersham so that it overlaps the bottom half of the satin loops.
3 (Ak) Sew another row of satin loops overlapping the bottom half of the pleats.
4 (Al) Thread petersham ribbon through the buckle to form a double bow and sew to the bottom of the buckram.
5 Hand stitch the cocarde to the hatband.

Aj   **Ak**   **Al**

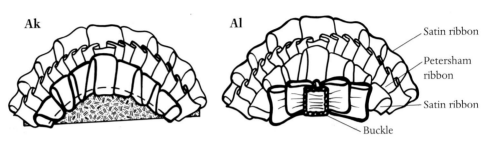

Satin ribbon
Petersham ribbon
Satin ribbon
Buckle

Dress ★★

The back-fastening dress (see back cover) has a dropped waist and a double gathered skirt. The bodice has a plastron which is edged with lace, ribbon and braid. The sleeves are full and tied at the wrists with ribbon. The sash fastens at the back with hooks and is decorated with ribbon rosettes at the front and a bow at the back.

Materials and notions

2.5m (98in) of lace and ribbon edging 4cm (1½in) deep. The decorative trim was purchased ready-sewn to a backing mesh. It consists of a row of gathered narrow lace, above which is a row of gathered ribbon and above that a final row of narrow gathered lace – all sewn to the soft backing mesh. Alternatively, obtain a length of 4cm (1½in) wide lace and sew a row of ribbon to the middle of the lace and then a row of narrow lace above the ribbon
30cm (12in) silk dupion 115cm (45in) wide
45cm (18in) fine silky fabric 115cm (45in) wide in a contrasting colour
15cm (6in) lining fabric 36cm (14in) wide – there is sufficient fabric in the amount given for the contrast fabric above, which could be used for the lining
60cm (24in) braid
1.3m (51in) lace 1cm (⅜in) wide
1.75cm (69in) satin ribbon 2mm (⅛in) wide
Sewing thread to match
Five buttons
Seven hooks and eyes

Pattern pieces There are nine pattern pieces for the dress, numbered A12 to A20.

Making instructions

1 (Am) Gather the plastron along the lines indicated on the pattern. Pull up the gathers until the plastron measures 6cm (2¼in) across. Tie off all ends.
2 R.s.f., sew the plastron to the bodice side fronts. Press the seams towards the side seams taking care not to flatten the plastron.
3 Using the bodice lining pattern as a guide mark the neckline on the plastron and sew a line of small stitches on the neckline. Cut away the surplus fabric.

Am

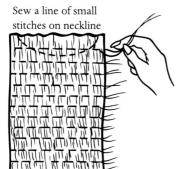

Sew a line of small stitches on neckline

The bodice front should now fit the bodice front lining pattern.

4 (An) Sew a length of ribbon and lace down either side of the plastron as indicated on the pattern. Repeat with the other side.

5 (An) Sew a length of braid just inside the ribbon.

6 (An) R.s.f., stitch the bodice shoulder seams. Press.

7 (An) Repeat with the lining.

8 (An) Gather a length of narrow lace and sew to the r.s. of neckline; the top of the lace is level with the raw edge of neck.

9 R.s.f., sew bodice back to bodice lining, from the neck down to the waist; repeat with the other side. Turn to the r.s. and press.

10 R.s.f., sew the neckband around neckline.

11 (Ao) Sew flat narrow lace to the cuffs as indicated on the pattern.

12 (Ap) With r.s.f., stitch the cuffs to the sleeves, press.

13 (Ap) Make the buttonholes as indicated.

14 (Ap) Neaten the lower raw edges of the cuffs and press towards the w.s. along the fold line.

15 Gather the sleeve headings and pull up to fit armholes.

16 With r.s.f., sew the sleeves to bodice armholes.

17 With r.s.f., sew the sleeve seam from the notch mark on the cuff towards the armhole, continue across the armhole seam and down the bodice side seam, press.

18 R.s.f., sew up the bodice lining side seam, press.

19 (Aq) Make a casing for the ribbon tie by sewing a row of stitching on either side of the buttonhole around each sleeve.

20 R.s.f., sew up the centre back seam on the skirt leaving a 3cm (1¼in) opening at the waist edge. Repeat with the skirt lining.

21 R.s.f., sew a length of trim to the bottom of the skirt. The top edge of the trim will be against the raw edge of the skirt hem.

22 With r.s.f., and enclosing the trim, sew the skirt to the skirt lining around the hem. Press and turn to the r.s.

23 Sew up the back seam of the overskirt using a French seam, leaving an opening at the waist edge. Press.

24 Turn up a narrow double hem on the overskirt.

25 With w.s. of trim against r.s. of overskirt, stitch a row of trim around the bottom hem of the overskirt.

26 Sew a row of narrow ribbon around the top edge of the trim, to cover the hem stitching.

27 Put the skirt inside the overskirt and line up the raw edges.

An

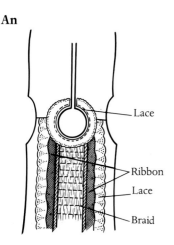

Lace
Ribbon
Lace
Braid

Ao

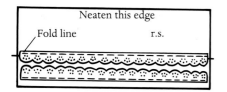

Neaten this edge
Fold line   r.s.

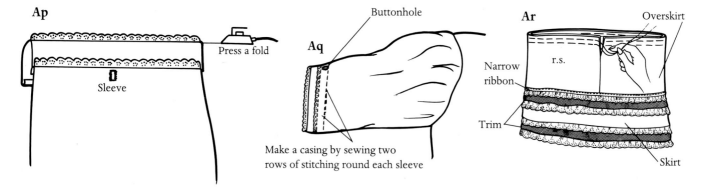

Ap

Press a fold

Sleeve

Aq

Buttonhole

Make a casing by sewing two rows of stitching round each sleeve

Ar

Overskirt
Narrow ribbon
r.s.
Trim
Skirt

As

28 (Ar) Stitch two rows of gathering stitches around the waist edge and pull up to fit the bodice waist, leaving a small overlap on the bodice for fastening.

29 With r.s.f., stitch the skirt to the bodice taking care not to catch the bodice lining.

30 Turn the edge of the bodice lining under and, enclosing all the raw edges, hand stitch the lining in place.

31 Turn the neck binding to the w.s., turn under a narrow hem and hand stitch.

32 Turn under a small hem on the bodice lining around the armholes and hand stitch to the sleeve headings.

33 Sew five hooks and eyes evenly spaced down the back opening. Optional: sew small beads or buttons on top of the hooks.

34 (As) Thread narrow ribbon through the sleeves, pull up to fit the wrists, and tie in bows.

Sash★

Materials and notions

1.05m (41in) soft petersham ribbon 4cm (1½in) wide – if necessary, wash to soften
1.05m (41in) satin ribbon 2.5cm (1in) wide
30cm (12in) braid

At

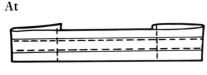

Au

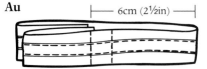

6cm (2½in)

Av

Pattern pieces None.

Making instructions

1 Cut a length of petersham ribbon 30cm (12in) long. Sew a length of satin ribbon down the centre of the petersham ribbon. Then sew a row of braid down the middle of the satin ribbon.

2 Measure your doll round the hip line and turn the ends of the ribbon under to fit. Stitch the ends in place and sew two hooks and eyes to fasten.

3 (At) Cut a 35cm (14in) length of petersham ribbon for the bow. Sew a length of satin ribbon down the middle of the petersham ribbon.

4 (Au) W.s.f., fold over 5cm (2in) at one end of the ribbon and stitch just inside the raw edge to form a loop, repeat with the other end of the ribbon.

5 (Au) W.s.f., fold the ribbon in half to form a loop and stitch 6cm (2½in) from the fold.

6 (Av; Aw) Place flat to make a double bow. Fold a 40cm (16in) piece of petersham ribbon in half lengthways, wrap it tightly round the middle of the bow and stitch together at the back of the bow.

7 Sew the bow to the back of the sash on top of the hooks.

8 To make a ribbon rosette cut a 20cm (8in) length of satin ribbon.

9 (Ax) Join the ends of the ribbon.

10 (Ay; Az) Make a lengthways fold turning over one-third of the ribbon. Sew a row of gathering stitches along the fold and pull up to form a rosette. You may like to decorate the centre of the rosette with a motif, small rose or fancy bead.

11 Repeat Instructions 8-10 with the second rosette.

12 Hand sew the rosettes to the front of the sash.

Aw

Ax

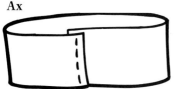

Ay

Az

Petticoat★★

The back-fastening petticoat is made of fine silk, and has a dropped waistline. The skirt and self-lined bodice are decorated with rows of tucks and lace.

Materials and notions
40cm (16in) fine silk 115cm (45in) wide
4.20m (166in) lace 1.5cm (⅝in) wide
Four hooks and eyes
Sewing thread to match

Pattern pieces There are four pattern pieces for the petticoat, numbered A21 to A24.

Making instructions

1 With r.s.f., sew up the back seam of the skirt leaving a 5cm (2in) opening at the waist edge.
2 (Aaa) Press up a narrow double hem and stitch in place.
3 (Aaa) Sew a row of flat lace on the r.s. at the hem line.
4 (Aaa) With w.s.f., press a fold 3cm (1¼ in) from the bottom of the hem.
5 (Aaa) Make the first tuck by sewing a row of stitching 1cm (⅜in) from the folded edge. Press the stitched tuck downwards.
6 (Aaa) Sew a row of lace above the tuck so that the bottom edge of the lace just covers the line of stitching making the tuck.
7 (Aaa) W.s.f., press a second fold 7cm (2¾in) from the bottom of the hem.
8 (Aaa) Make the second tuck by sewing a row of stitching 1cm (⅜in) from the fold. Press the second tuck downwards.
9 (Aaa) Sew a row of lace above the second tuck with the bottom edge of the lace just covering the stitching line.
10 (Abb) Sew rows of tucks and lace on the bodice front as indicated on the pattern. Press.
11 R.s.f., sew the bodice shoulder seams, press.
12 Repeat with the lining.
13 (Acc) With r.s.f., sew the lining to the bodice up the back opening, around the neck and down the other back opening.
14 (Acc) With r.s.f., sew bodice to lining around armholes.
15 Clip seams and turn to the r.s. by pulling the backs through the shoulders. Press.
16 (Add) Sew two rows of gathering stitches around the skirt waist and pull up to fit the bodice waist leaving a small overlap on the bodice for fastening.
17 With r.s.f., and raw edges level, stitch the skirt to bodice around the waist taking care not to catch the bodice lining.
18 Turn under a narrow hem on the bodice lining and hand stitch to the petticoat waist.
19 Sew four hooks and eyes to fasten the petticoat back.

Aaa
Stitching guide for petticoat skirt

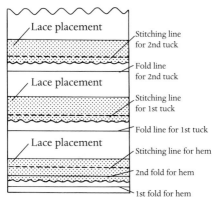

Lace placement
Stitching line for 2nd tuck
Fold line for 2nd tuck
Lace placement
Stitching line for 1st tuck
Fold line for 1st tuck
Lace placement
Stitching line for hem
2nd fold for hem
1st fold for hem

Abb

Diagram of folds for tucks on petticoat front
Stitch together here

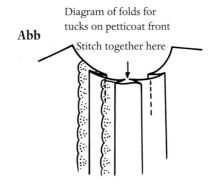

Acc

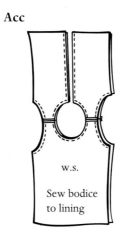

w.s.

Sew bodice to lining

Add

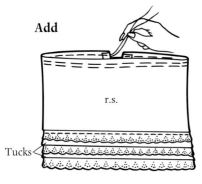

r.s.

Tucks

Camisole & Bloomers★

Aee

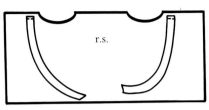

Aff

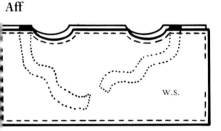

Folding sequence for front straps

Agg

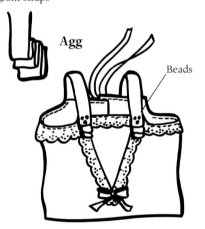

Beads

Ahh

Casings

The lined camisole is lace trimmed with ribbon straps. It fastens at the back with ribbon ties. The knee-length bloomers are self-lined. They are gathered at the waist and knees with ribbon ties.

Bloomers are named after Mrs Amelia Bloomer (1818-1894), a U.S. social reformer who campaigned to free women from wearing restrictive clothing.

Materials and notions

30cm (12in) fine silk 115cm (45in) wide – lining silk is suitable
1.30m (51in) lace 1cm (⅜in) wide
30cm (12in) ribbon 1cm (⅜in) wide for the shoulder straps
2m (78in) ribbon 2mm (⅛in) wide
Sewing thread to match

Pattern pieces There is one pattern piece for the camisole, numbered A25, and one pattern piece for the bloomers, numbered A26.

Making instructions – Camisole

1 Cut two 15cm (6in) pieces of 1cm (⅜in) wide ribbon for the shoulder straps.
2 (Aee) With raw edges level tack the ribbon shoulder straps to the r.s. of the back on notches.
3 (Aff) R.s.f., sew the camisole to the lining all round the edge leaving an opening along one back edge for turning.
4 Clip, turn to the r.s. and press.
5 Sew a V of lace on the front along lace placement line.
6 Sew a row of flat lace around the top of the camisole making small pleats in the lace where the straps join the fabric.
7 (Agg) Make three small loops at the end of the shoulder strap ribbon and hand stitch to the camisole front. Hand stitch small beads to front of straps.
8 (Agg) Hand stitch a bow of narrow ribbon to the bottom of the lace V.
9 Close the opening used for turning and sew ribbon ties to the back opening.

Making instructions – Bloomers

1 Make two small buttonholes on the front of the bloomer legs as marked on the pattern. Do not make buttonholes on the lining pieces.
2 R.s.f., sew up the inside leg seams. Press.
3 Matching seams and, with r.s.f., sew crotch seam, leaving a small opening at the top of the back to thread the ribbon ties through. Press.
4 Repeat Instructions 1-2 with the lining.
5 With r.s.f., sew the lining to the bloomers around the waist edge. Turn to the r.s. and press.
6 (Ahh) Make a casing around the waist by sewing a row of stitching 1cm (⅜in) from the waist edge.
7 Press a narrow hem to the inside on the bottom of the leg and on the leg lining. Stitch in place enclosing the raw edges.
8 Sew a row of flat lace around the bottom of the leg. Sew a second row above the first row.
9 Make a casing by sewing a row of stitching 1cm (⅜in) above the lace.
10 Thread narrow ribbon through the casing, pull up to fit the doll's leg and tie in a bow.
11 Repeat Instructions 7-10 with the other leg.
12 Thread narrow ribbon through the waist.

Socks★

The socks are hand knitted in cotton.

Materials
One ball No. 8 cotton perlé
One pair 2mm knitting needles
One pair 1.5mm knitting needles
Sewing-up needle

Making instructions
See page 9 for abbreviations.
With 1.5mm needles cast on 40 sts
Knit 8 rows of k1, p1, rib
Change to 2mm needles and continue as follows:
Row 1: K2tog, k7, k2tog, k8, k2tog, k8, k2tog, k7, k2tog (35 sts)
Row 2: P
Row 3: K
Row 4: P
Row 5: K7, yon, k2tog, k8, yon, k2tog, k8, yon, k2tog, k6
Row 6: P
Row 7: K6, yon, k2tog, yon, k2tog, k6, yon, k2tog, yon, k2tog, k6, yon, k2tog, yon, k2tog, k5
Row 8: P
Row 9: K
Row 10: P
Row 11: K
Row 12: P
Row 13: K12, yon, k2tog, k8, yon, k2tog, k11
Row 14: P
Row 15: K11, yon, k2tog, yon, k2tog, k6, yon, k2tog, yon, k2tog, k10
Row 16: P
Row 17: K
Row 18: P
Row 19: K
Row 20: P
Row 21: K
Rep. from row 2 to row 20 once more

Foot shaping
K23, turn (leaving 12 sts on left needle)
P11, turn
Continue in st.st. on these centre 11 sts, and knit a further 10 rows (ending on a p row)

K11, pick up 7 sts along side of foot and k the 12 sts from the left needle
P30, pick up 7 sts along the side of foot and p the 12 sts from the left needle (49 sts)
Knit 4 rows in st.st.

Heel shaping
K2tog, k20, k2tog, k1, k2tog, k20, k2tog
P2tog, p18, p2tog, p1, p2tog, p18, p2tog
K2tog, k16, k2tog, k1, k2tog, k16, k2tog
P2tog, p14, p2tog, p1, p2tog, p14, p2tog
K2tog, k12, k2tog, k1, k2tog, k12, k2tog
P2tog, p10, p2tog, p1, p2tog, p10, p2tog
Cast off

Sew up sole and leg seam. Repeat the instructions for the other sock.

Shoes★

The shoes are made of soft leather. They have rosettes on the fronts and ribbon ties at the ankles.

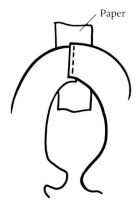

Aii

Paper

Materials and notions
12cm (4¾in) square soft leather
10cm (4in) square stiff leather for the soles and heels
Glue (contact adhesive)
Stiff cardboard for the insoles, picture mounting quality
Thin card for the infills
25cm (10in) ricrac braid
40cm (12in) ribbon 2mm (⅛in) wide

Pattern pieces There are five pattern pieces for the shoes, numbered A27 to A31.

Making instructions
1 (Aii) Overlap the back seam and glue in place. Stitch when the glue has dried. If your machine does not travel freely over the leather place a piece of paper under the seam while sewing.
2 (Ajj) Put a layer of glue on the shaded area around the edge of the card insole. Put the insole, sticky side facing outwards, into the shoe and bend the bottom of the leather upper smoothly down over the glued edge of the card sole. Hold in place whilst the glue dries.
3 Stick the card infill between the edges of the leather on the card sole.
4 Stick the leather sole in place.
5 Stick the heel to the sole. Place a weight on the shoe until the glue has dried.
6 (Akk) Gather half of the ricrac braid along the bottom curves and pull up to form a rosette. Hand sew to the front of the shoe.
7 (All) Punch two holes in the straps and thread half the narrow ribbon through.

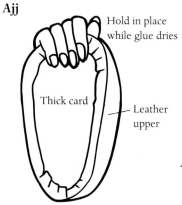

Ajj

Hold in place while glue dries

Thick card

Leather upper

Akk

All

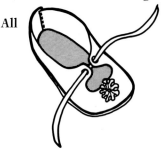

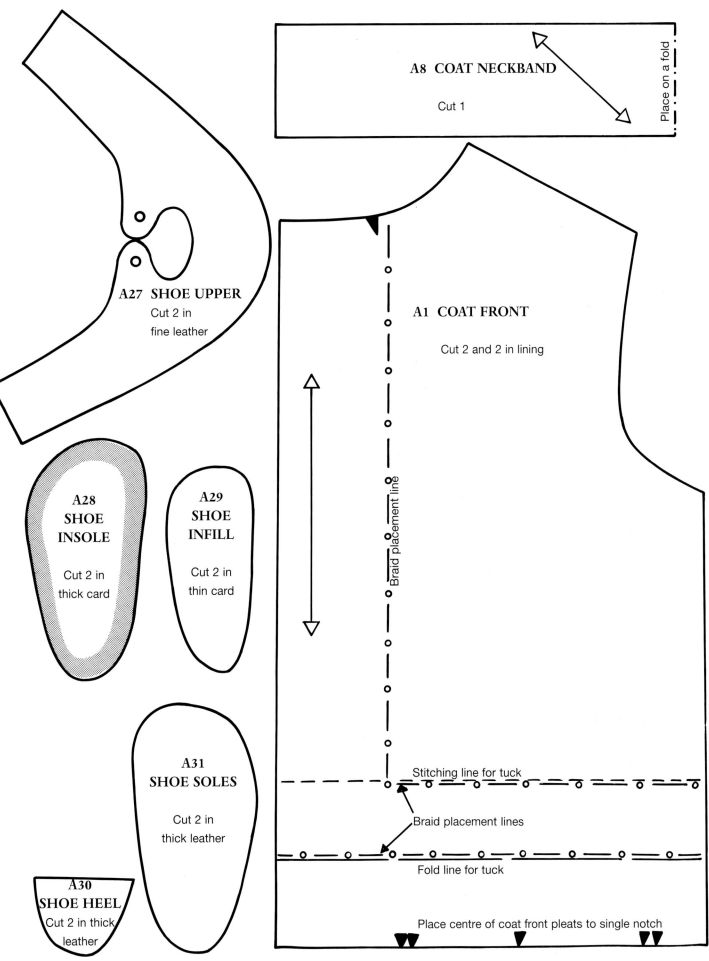

A8 COAT NECKBAND

Cut 1

Place on a fold

A27 SHOE UPPER
Cut 2 in
fine leather

A1 COAT FRONT

Cut 2 and 2 in lining

Braid placement line

**A28
SHOE
INSOLE**

Cut 2 in
thick card

**A29
SHOE
INFILL**

Cut 2 in
thin card

**A31
SHOE SOLES**

Cut 2 in
thick leather

**A30
SHOE HEEL**
Cut 2 in thick
leather

Stitching line for tuck

Braid placement lines

Fold line for tuck

Place centre of coat front pleats to single notch

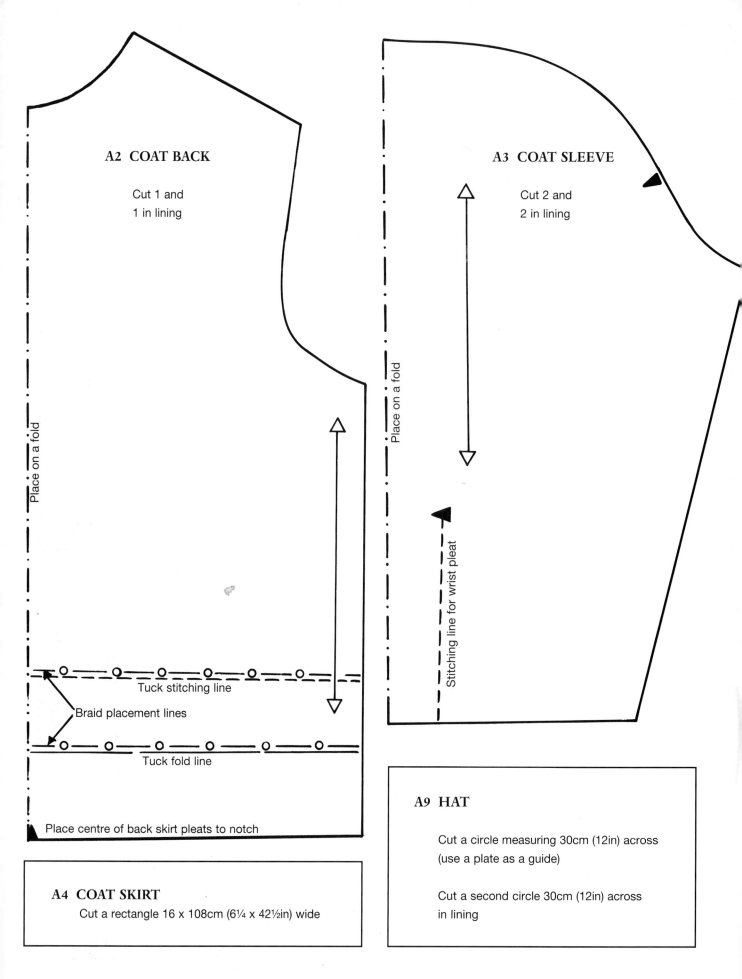

A2 COAT BACK

Cut 1 and
1 in lining

Place on a fold

Tuck stitching line

Braid placement lines

Tuck fold line

Place centre of back skirt pleats to notch

A3 COAT SLEEVE

Cut 2 and
2 in lining

Place on a fold

Stitching line for wrist pleat

A4 COAT SKIRT
Cut a rectangle 16 x 108cm (6¼ x 42½in) wide

A9 HAT

Cut a circle measuring 30cm (12in) across
(use a plate as a guide)

Cut a second circle 30cm (12in) across
in lining

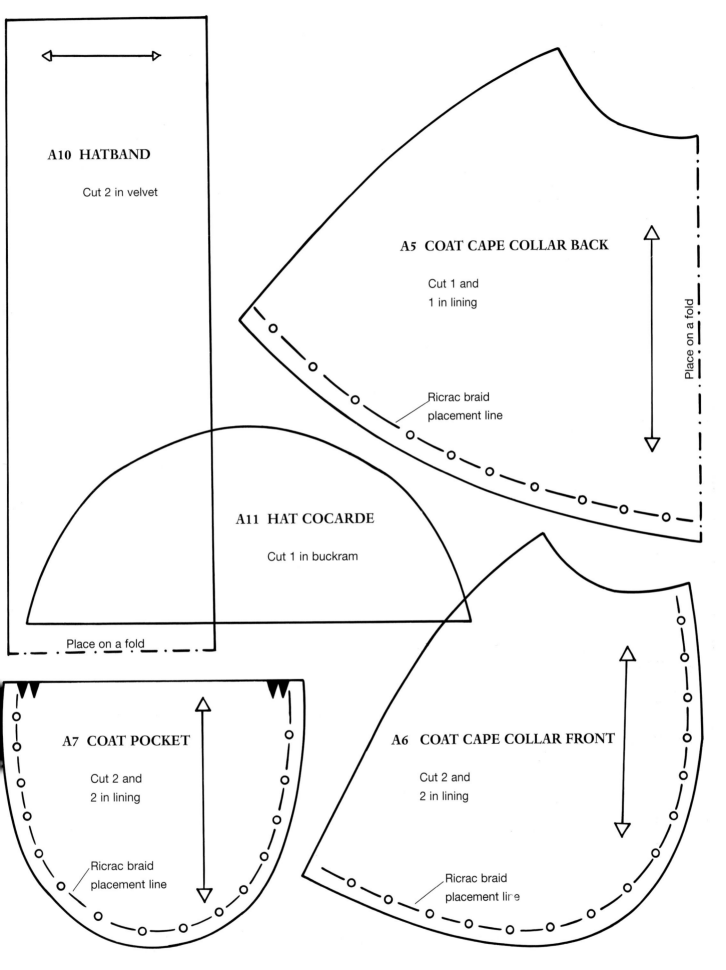

A10 HATBAND

Cut 2 in velvet

A5 COAT CAPE COLLAR BACK

Cut 1 and
1 in lining

Place on a fold

Ricrac braid
placement line

A11 HAT COCARDE

Cut 1 in buckram

Place on a fold

A7 COAT POCKET

Cut 2 and
2 in lining

Ricrac braid
placement line

A6 COAT CAPE COLLAR FRONT

Cut 2 and
2 in lining

Ricrac braid
placement line

73

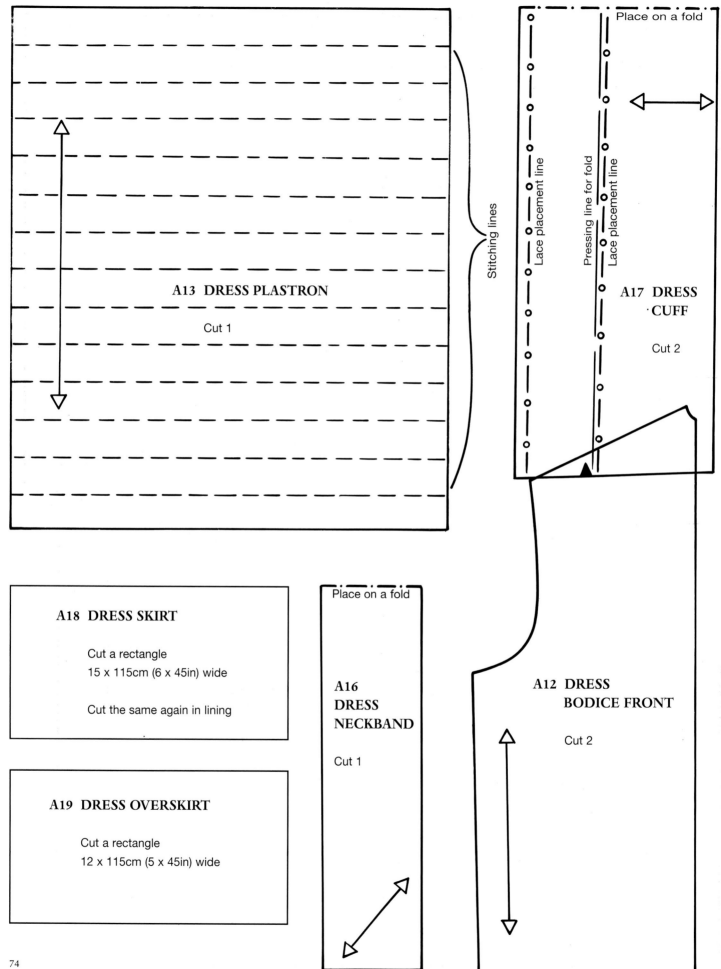

A13 DRESS PLASTRON

Cut 1

Stitching lines

Place on a fold

Lace placement line

Pressing line for fold

Lace placement line

A17 DRESS CUFF

Cut 2

A18 DRESS SKIRT

Cut a rectangle
15 x 115cm (6 x 45in) wide

Cut the same again in lining

A19 DRESS OVERSKIRT

Cut a rectangle
12 x 115cm (5 x 45in) wide

Place on a fold

A16 DRESS NECKBAND

Cut 1

A12 DRESS BODICE FRONT

Cut 2

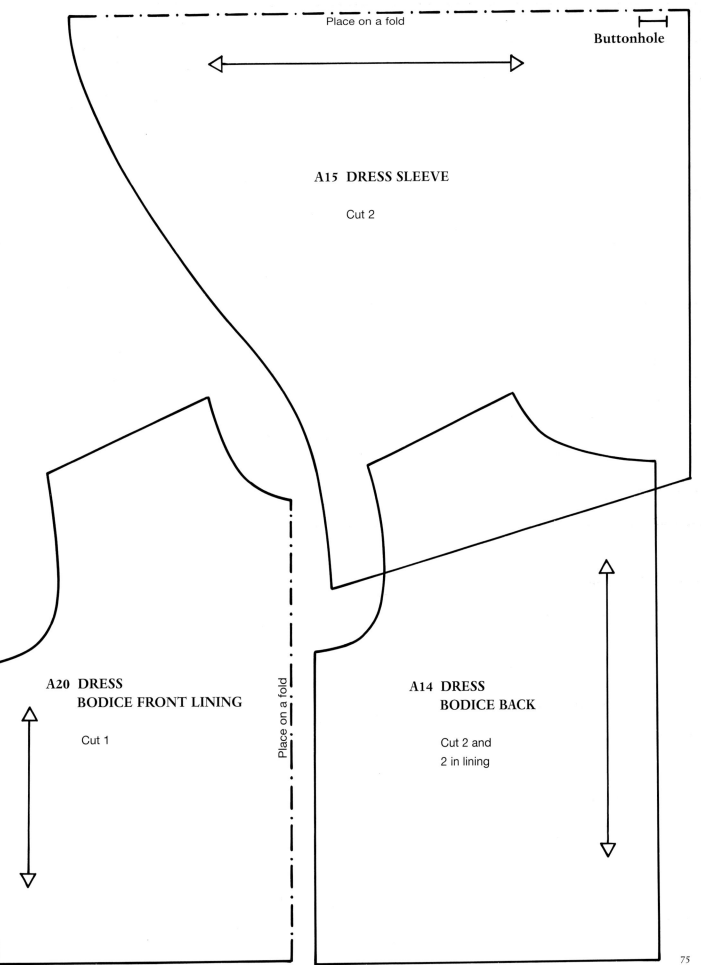

Place on a fold

Buttonhole

A15 DRESS SLEEVE

Cut 2

**A20 DRESS
BODICE FRONT LINING**

Cut 1

Place on a fold

**A14 DRESS
BODICE BACK**

Cut 2 and
2 in lining

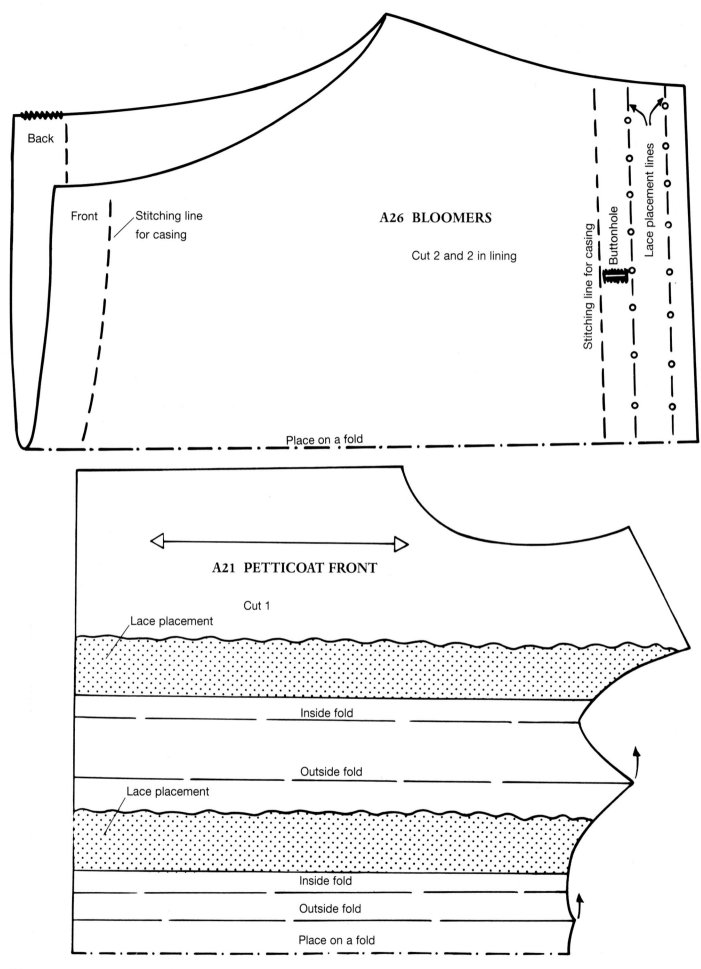

A26 BLOOMERS

Cut 2 and 2 in lining

Back

Front

Stitching line for casing

Stitching line for casing

Buttonhole

Lace placement lines

Place on a fold

A21 PETTICOAT FRONT

Cut 1

Lace placement

Inside fold

Outside fold

Lace placement

Inside fold

Outside fold

Place on a fold

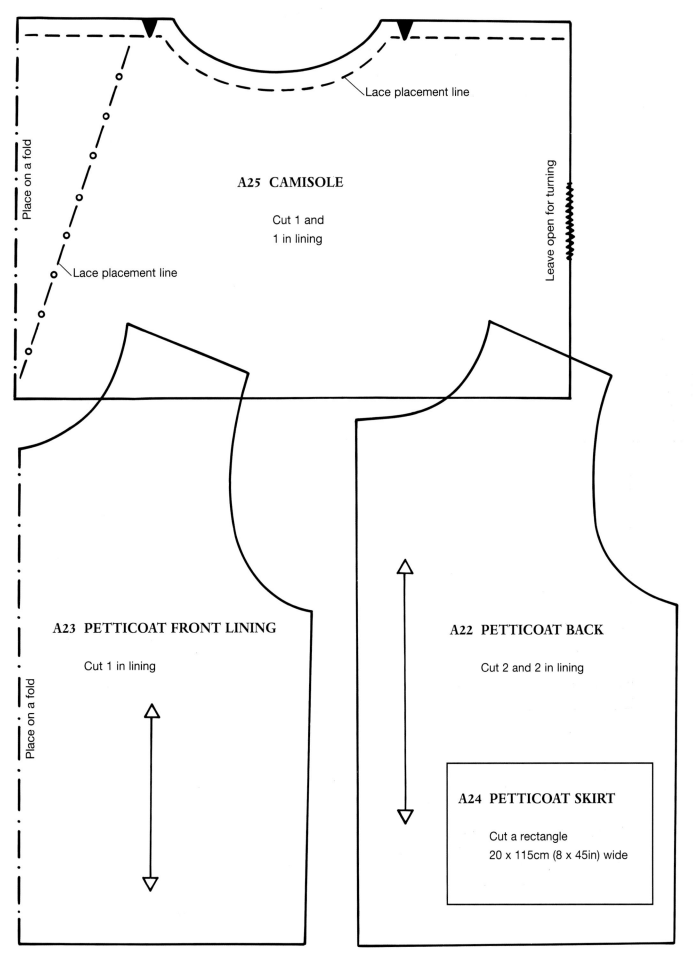

A25 CAMISOLE

Cut 1 and
1 in lining

Lace placement line

Place on a fold

Lace placement line

Leave open for turning

A23 PETTICOAT FRONT LINING

Cut 1 in lining

Place on a fold

A22 PETTICOAT BACK

Cut 2 and 2 in lining

A24 PETTICOAT SKIRT

Cut a rectangle
20 x 115cm (8 x 45in) wide

MARC

Sailor suit

The boy doll is a German reproduction doll. He has a porcelain head with moulded hair and a composition body. He is dressed in a typical sailor suit which consists of a cotton reefer jacket with a sailor collar and midi-length cotton trousers. He wears a sailor hat and striped socks.

If you prefer to dress a girl doll in a sailor suit, use the trousers waistband and replace the trousers with a pleated skirt. The underpants will need to fasten at the back and may be trimmed with lace. The vest could be embroidered and trimmed with narrow lace. The sailor suit first became a popular outfit for small boys in 1846 when the young Prince of Wales wore one on board the Royal yacht. The craze soon spread across England, throughout Europe and beyond. As time went on it became more elaborate and by the 1880s it had even extended to girls' wear and included a short pleated skirt. This fashion proved so popular that it has remained to the present day. Marc's outfit consists of jacket, trousers, hat, vest, underpants, socks and shoes.

Dimensions

Height: 46cm (18in)

Circumference of head: 28cm (11in)

Waist: 24cm (9½in)

Neck: 15cm (6in)

Pattern pieces There are 21 pattern pieces for Marc's entire outfit, numbered M1 to M21 and printed on pages 88-93.

Note: All markings for braid placement may be transferred to the fabric using dressmaker's carbon paper.

Reefer jacket★★

The jacket is single-breasted. It is lined and has contrasting collar, pockets and cuffs which are decorated with braid.

Materials and notions

25cm (10in) medium-weight white cotton 115cm (45in) wide
25cm (10in) lightweight cotton for the lining 115cm (45in) wide
Blue cotton fabric and lining – there is sufficient fabric in the amount given for the trousers (page 82) for the contrast collar, pockets and cuffs
2m (79in) white Russia braid
1m (39in) blue Russia braid
Five small buttons
Sewing threads to match

Pattern pieces There are seven pattern pieces for the reefer jacket, numbered M1 to M7.

Making instructions

1 Neaten all edges.
2 With r.s.f., join the shoulder seams and press open.
3 (Ma) R.s.f., sew the contrasting cuffs to the sleeves. Press cuffs downwards.
4 Sew the braid to the cuffs as marked on the pattern.
5 R.s.f., sew the pocket to the pocket lining around the curved edge, clip the seam, turn to the right side and press. Repeat with the second pocket.
6 Sew the braid on the r.s. of the pockets as indicated on the pattern.
7 (Mb) With r.s.f., and the curved edge of the pocket facing upwards stitch the pocket to the jacket front on stitching line.
8 Press the curved edge of the pocket downwards and catch the top side edges to the jacket by hand. Repeat with the second pocket.
9 With r.s.f., sew the sleeve heading to the jacket. Repeat with the second sleeve.
10 R.s.f., stitch the sleeve lining to the sleeve at the wrist edge. Repeat with the second sleeve.
11 (Mc) With r.s.f. and seams matching, sew up the jacket side seam, continue along the sleeve seam and then along the sleeve lining. Press and turn to the r.s. tucking the sleeve lining inside the sleeve. Repeat with the other side.
12 R.s.f., join the lining shoulder seams. Press.
13 R.s.f., join the lining side seams. Press.

Ma

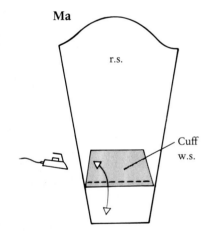

r.s.

Cuff
w.s.

Mb

r.s.

w.s.

Mc

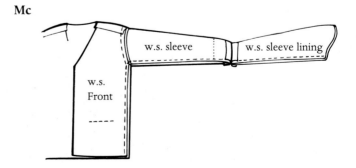

w.s. sleeve   w.s. sleeve lining

w.s.
Front

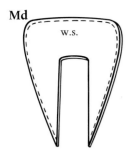

Md

w.s.

14 (Md) With r.s.f., sew the collar to the collar lining around the outside edge. Clip the seam, turn to the right side and press.

15 Sew the braid to the right side of the collar as marked on the pattern.

16 (Me) With the w.s. of the collar against the r.s. of the jacket and matching notches, tack the collar to the neck of the jacket.

17 With r.s.f., stitch the jacket to the jacket lining (enclosing the collar) around the neck edge, down the front, around the bottom and back up the other front. Clip seams and turn to the right side through the armholes. Press.

18 Sew one row of white braid to the r.s. of the neck insert on placement line.

19 With r.s.f., stitch neck insert to neck insert lining leaving an opening for turning.

20 Clip seams, turn to the right side and press. Close the opening with hand stitching.

21 Stitch the insert in place matching notches.

22 (Mf) Hand stitch the sleeve linings to the lining around the armholes.

23 (Mg) The collar will lie flatter if you sew a row of stitching around the neck edge beneath the collar.

24 Sew small buttons to the front as indicated on the pattern and make corresponding buttonholes to match.

25 Sew two buttons as decoration on each cuff.

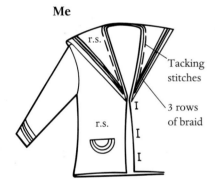

Me

r.s.

Tacking stitches

3 rows of braid

r.s.

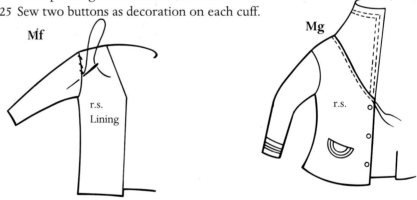

Mf

r.s. Lining

Mg

r.s.

Sailor trousers★

The trousers are midi-length, ending just below the knee. They are lined and have a back fastening. The legs are trimmed with braid down the sides.

Materials and notions
25cm (10in) blue medium-weight cotton 115cm (45in) wide
25cm (10in) lightweight blue cotton for lining 70cm (27½in) wide
1m (39in) white Russia braid
50cm (20in) blue Russia braid
One hook and eye
Sewing thread to match

Pattern pieces There are two pattern pieces for the trousers, numbered M8 and M9.

Making instructions
1 Neaten all edges.
2 (Mh) Sew the Russia braid to the r.s. of the leg along the lines indicated on the pattern – two white rows with a blue row between them.
3 Repeat with the other leg.
4 R.s.f., sew up the leg seam. Press.

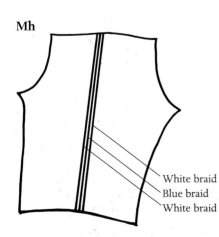

Mh

White braid
Blue braid
White braid

5 Repeat with the other leg.

6 Matching seams and with r.s.f., sew the crotch seam leaving an opening at the waist edge. Clip seams and press.

7 Repeat Instructions 4-6 with the lining.

8 Insert the lining and tack to the trousers at the waist edge.

9 With r.s.f., sew the waistband to the waist edge of the trousers.

10 Fold the waistband to the w.s. turn under a narrow hem and hand stitch in place.

11 Hand stitch round the back opening and sew a hook and eye to fasten the waistband.

12 Adjust the leg length to suit your doll by turning up a hem on the trouser leg and the lining, enclosing the raw edges and press.

13 Slip stitch round the bottom by hand, and then repeat with the other leg.

Sailor hat★

The main part of the hat is white, and the band is blue with white braid and embroidery.

Note: Check your doll's head circumference with the pattern and adjust the pattern if necessary.

Materials and notions

White cotton and lining – there is sufficient fabric for the hat in the amount given for the jacket (page 80) and sufficient fabric for the hatband in the amount given for the trousers (opposite)

15cm (6in) blue petersham ribbon 2.5cm (1in) wide

30cm (12in) white Russia braid

Sewing threads to match

White embroidery thread

Pattern pieces There are three pattern pieces for the hat, numbered M10 to M12.

Making instructions

1 With r.s.f., join the two circles of the hat together around the outer edge. Clip the seam, turn to the right side and press.

2 R.s. f., join the two circles of the hat lining together around the outer edge, clip the seam and press.

3 Insert the lining into the hat and tack in place around the inner edge.

4 Optional: embroider the hatband.

5 (Mi) Sew a row of braid around the hatband as indicated on the pattern.

6 (Mi) Tack the petersham to the hatband.

7 (Mi) R.s.f., sew up the back seam of the hatband.

8 With r.s.f., sew the hatband to the hat through all layers.

9 Press the hatband towards the inside just below the braid, turn a narrow hem to the w.s. and hand stitch to the lining.

Mi

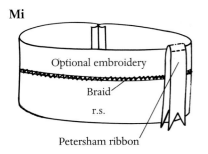

Optional embroidery

Braid

r.s.

Petersham ribbon

Vest★

The vest is half-lined, has short sleeves and is fastened at the front.

Note: if your doll has an all porcelain or fabric body, you may need to make the vest open all the way down the front to make dressing easier. If so, cut the lining the same size as the vest.

Materials and notions
25 cm (10 in) fine woollen fabric 115 cm (45 in) wide
Three small buttons
Sewing thread to match

Pattern pieces There are three pattern pieces for the vest, numbered M13 to M15.

Making instructions
1 Neaten all raw edges.
2 With r.s.f., sew the shoulder seams. Repeat with the lining.
3 R.s.f., sew up the centre front seam leaving the neck edge open (see notches)
4 (Mj) R.s.f., sew lining to vest up the front facing around the neck and down the other facing. Clip seams, turn to r.s. and press.
5 With r.s.f., sew sleeve heading to vest and lining easing the head of the sleeve round as you sew.
6 Repeat with the other sleeve.
7 R.s.f. and seams matching, sew up the sleeve seam across armhole seam and down the side seam. Press.
8 Repeat with the other side.
9 Press up a single hem to the w.s. around the bottom of the vest and stitch in place.
10 Turn up a narrow single hem around the bottom of each sleeve and stitch in place.
11 Make three buttonholes at neck opening.
12 Sew three buttons opposite the buttonholes.

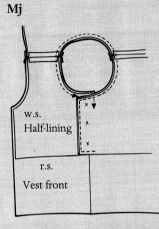

Mj

w.s.
Half-lining

r.s.
Vest front

Underpants★

The underpants are knee length and fasten with two buttons at the front. The tapes at the back adjust the waist size.

Materials and notions
Woollen fabric – there is sufficient fabric for the underpants in the amount given for the vest (above)
47 cm (18½ in) narrow white tape
Two small buttons
Sewing thread to match

Pattern pieces There is one pattern piece for the underpants, numbered M16.

Mk

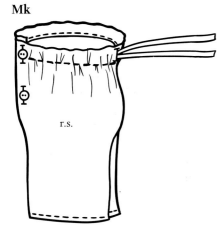

r.s.

Making instructions

1　Neaten all raw edges.
2　With r.s.f., sew the leg seam and press.
3　Repeat with the other leg.
4　R.s.f. and matching seams, sew the crotch seam, leaving an opening at the front – see notches. Press.
5　Press the facings to the w.s. Make two buttonholes on the front and one at the centre back as marked on the pattern.
6　Turn a 1.5cm (½in) single hem to the w.s. at the waist edge and stitch in place.
7　Turn up a narrow single hem at the bottom of the legs and stitch in place.
8　Thread narrow tape through the waistband, pull a loop of tape out through the centre back buttonhole and cut in the centre of the loop.
9　Stitch the ends of the tape in place at the front opening.
10　(Mk) Sew two buttons opposite the buttonholes at the front opening.

Socks★

The socks are hand-knitted in cotton.

Materials

One ball No. 8 cotton perlé in white for the main colour
One ball No. 8 cotton perlé in royal blue as the contrast colour
One pair 2mm knitting needles
Sewing-up needle

Making instructions

See page 9 for abbreviations.
Cast on 40 sts, using the white cotton and knit 8 rows in k1, p1, rib
Next row: K, inc 1 st in every 10th st (44 sts)
Next row: P
Change to the blue cotton and k
Next row: P
The pattern consists of two rows of white and two rows of blue knitted in st.st.
Continue knitting the striped pattern until you have completed the 9th blue stripe.
Keeping the stripes correct, shape the ankle by k2 tog at the beg and end of the next 2 k rows (40 sts) ending with a blue p row.

Foot shaping

K27 sts, turn, p14 sts
Keeping the stripes correct k a further 15 rows of st.st. on these centre 14 sts, ending with a white k row.
Pick up and k9 sts along the side of the foot, then k the 13 sts from the left needle
P36 sts, then pick up 9 sts purlwise along the side of the foot and p the 13 sts from the left needle (58 sts)
Continue in st.st. using the white cotton, for a further 8 rows

Sole shaping (continue knitting in white)

K2tog, k25, k2tog, k2tog, k25, k2tog
P2tog, p23, p2tog, p2tog, p23, p2tog
K2tog, k21, k2tog, k2tog, k21, k2tog
P2tog, p19, p2tog, p2tog, p19, p2tog
K2tog, k17, k2tog, k2tog, k17, k2tog
Cast off

Sew up the centre sole and back seam.
Repeat the instructions for the second sock.

Shoes★

The shoes have an ankle strap fastening and a cut-out design on the fronts.
Note: a backing of paper or stitch-and-tear Vilene will allow the leather to feed freely through the machine.

Materials and notions
12cm (5in) fine white leather 24cm (9½in) wide for the uppers
13cm (5in) thicker leather 8cm (3in) wide for the soles and heels
Two small buckles
Clear glue (contact adhesive)
Sewing thread to match
A small piece of cardboard, picture mounting quality
Thin card for the infills
Several clothes pegs

Pattern pieces There are five pattern pieces for the shoes, numbered M17 to M21.

Ml

Stitch up one side seam, around front of shoe and down other side seam

Making instructions
1 Stick the strap in place, w.s. of strap to r.s. of shoe back. Allow the glue to dry and stitch.
2 Repeat with the other strap.
3 (Ml) Stick the side seams, w.s. of shoe front to r.s. of shoe back. Allow the glue to dry. Stitch up one side seam around the front of the foot and down the other side seam.
4 Repeat Instructions 1-3 with the other shoe.
5 Put a layer of glue around the shaded area of the cardboard sole and a layer around the inside sole edge of the shoe.
6 Using the doll's foot as a last, put the shoe on to the foot, insert the card sole into the shoe (sticky side out!).
7 Bend the glued portion of the leather over on to the card, remove the shoe from the foot and hold the pieces in place until dry with clothes pegs.
8 Repeat Instructions 5-7 with the other shoe.
9 Cut two thin card soles the size of the non-shaded area on the pattern piece and stick as infills between the leather on the card soles of the shoes.
10 Stick the leather soles to the shoes.
11 Stick the heels to the shoes.
12 Hand sew the buckles in place.

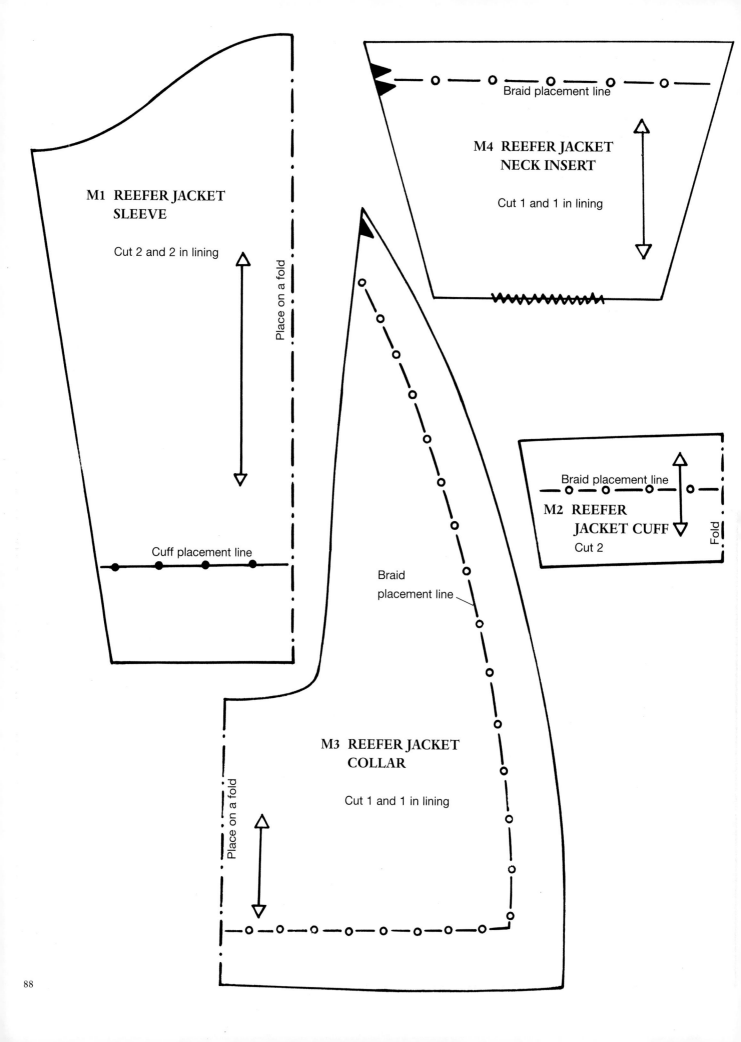

M1 REEFER JACKET
SLEEVE

Cut 2 and 2 in lining

Place on a fold

Cuff placement line

M4 REEFER JACKET
NECK INSERT

Cut 1 and 1 in lining

Braid placement line

Braid placement line

M2 REEFER
JACKET CUFF
Cut 2

Fold

Braid
placement line

M3 REEFER JACKET
COLLAR

Cut 1 and 1 in lining

Place on a fold

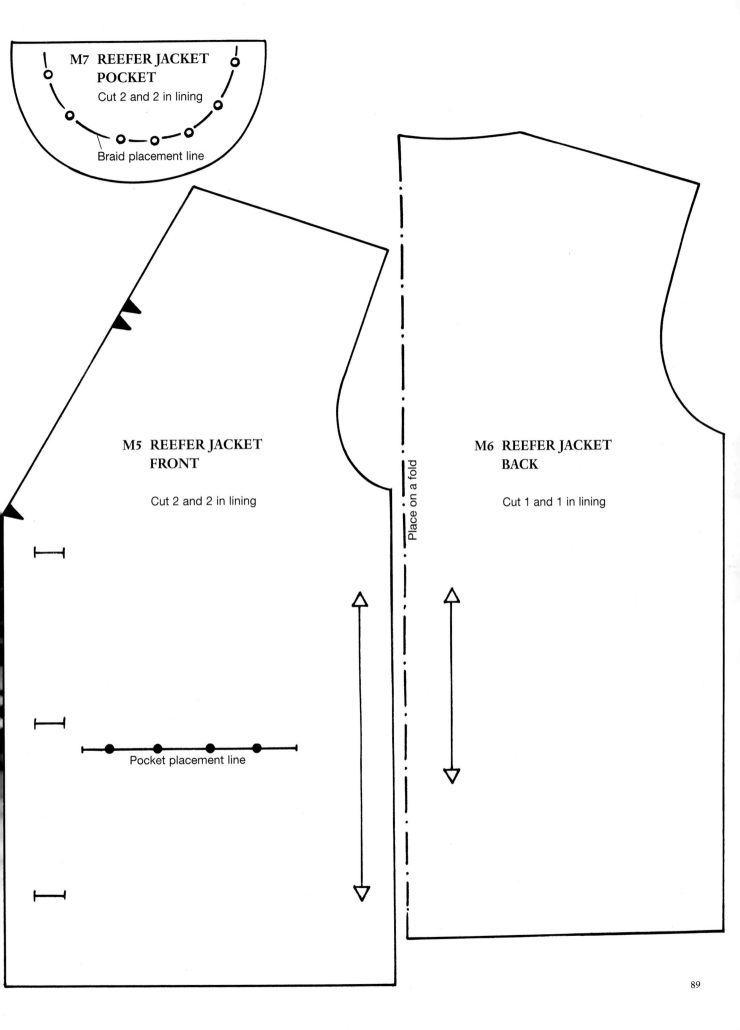

M7 REEFER JACKET POCKET

Cut 2 and 2 in lining

Braid placement line

M5 REEFER JACKET FRONT

Cut 2 and 2 in lining

Pocket placement line

M6 REEFER JACKET BACK

Cut 1 and 1 in lining

Place on a fold

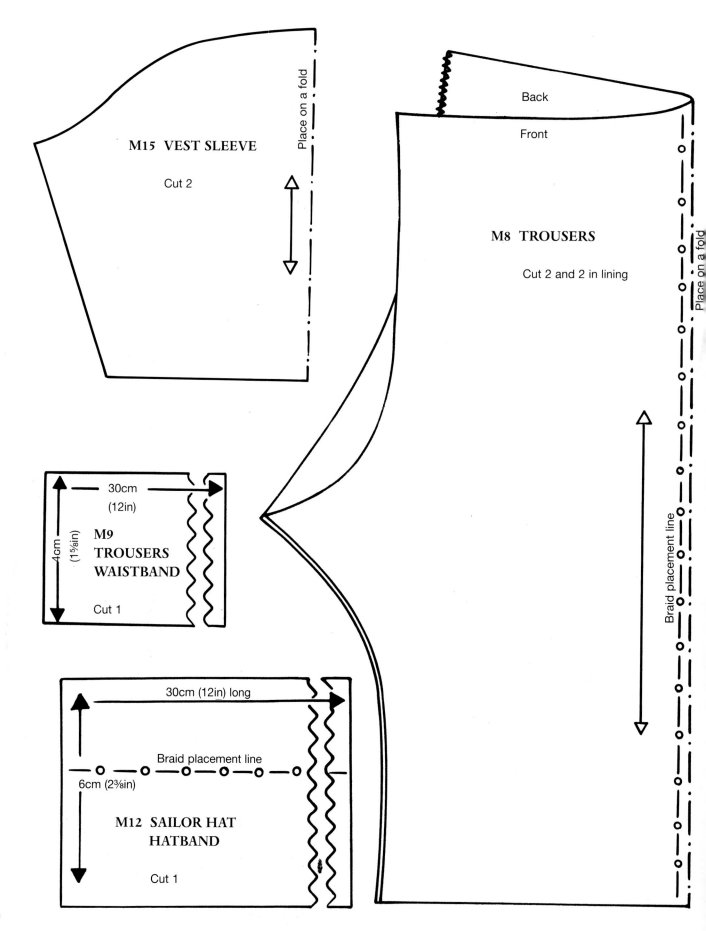

M15 VEST SLEEVE

Cut 2

Place on a fold

M8 TROUSERS

Cut 2 and 2 in lining

Back

Front

Place on a fold

Braid placement line

30cm
(12in)

4cm
(1⅝in)

**M9
TROUSERS
WAISTBAND**

Cut 1

30cm (12in) long

Braid placement line

6cm (2⅜in)

**M12 SAILOR HAT
HATBAND**

Cut 1

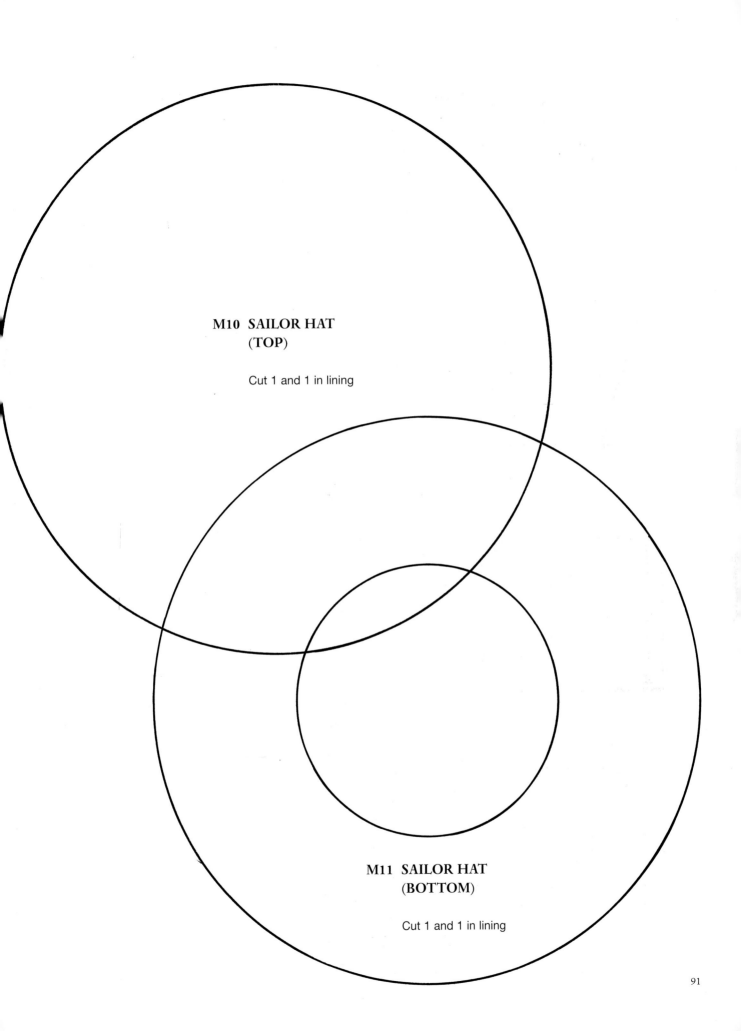

**M10 SAILOR HAT
(TOP)**

Cut 1 and 1 in lining

**M11 SAILOR HAT
(BOTTOM)**

Cut 1 and 1 in lining

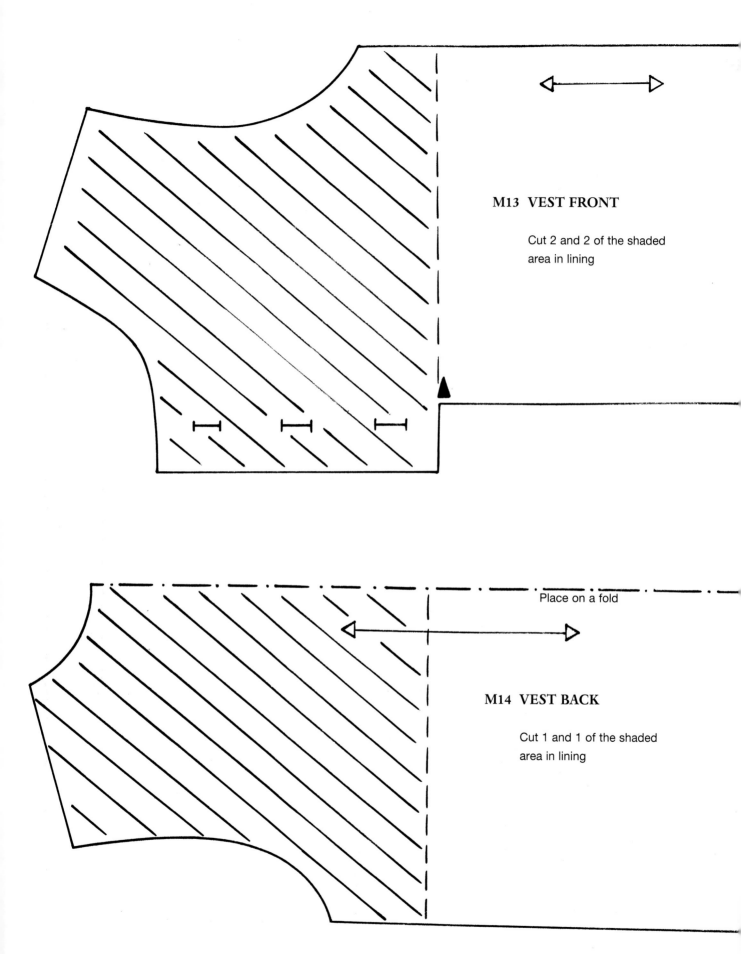

M13 VEST FRONT

Cut 2 and 2 of the shaded
area in lining

Place on a fold

M14 VEST BACK

Cut 1 and 1 of the shaded
area in lining

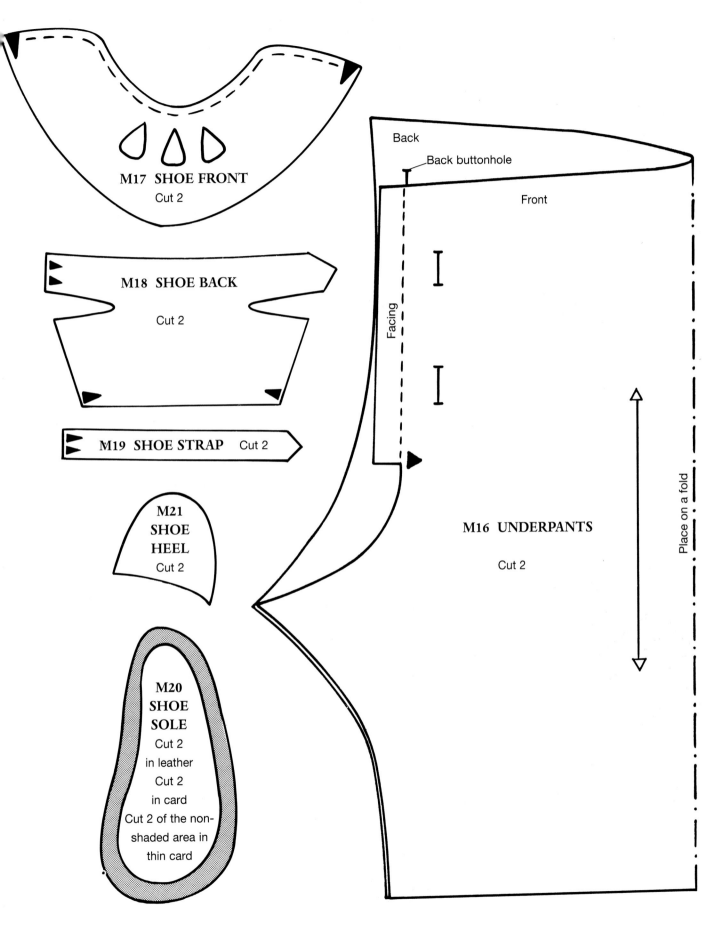

M17 SHOE FRONT
Cut 2

M18 SHOE BACK

Cut 2

M19 SHOE STRAP   Cut 2

M21
SHOE
HEEL
Cut 2

M20
SHOE
SOLE
Cut 2
in leather
Cut 2
in card
Cut 2 of the non-
shaded area in
thin card

Back

Back buttonhole

Front

Facing

Place on a fold

M16 UNDERPANTS

Cut 2

HERMIONE

Elegant outdoor wear

This doll is a porcelain reproduction fashion doll taken from an original by François Gaultier. She has a porcelain head on a composition body. The body proportions of a fashion doll resemble those of an adult – the waist is more pronounced, the head is smaller and the limbs are long and lean. The clothes for this type of doll usually have a tailored look to them. By the 1870s the shape of skirts had changed from the full gathered skirt supported by a crinoline to a skirt which was flat at the front with the fullness at the back. This fullness was enhanced by a bustle tied around the waist beneath the skirt. Hermione's outfit consists of bodice and overskirt, skirt, bustle, lace jabot and neckband, hat, waist petticoat, pantaloons, chemisette, lace mittens, parasol, socks and boots.

Dimensions

Height: 46cm (18in)

Circumference of head: 25cm (10in)

Waist: 18cm (7in)

Neck: 14cm (5½in)

Bodice & overskirt★★★

Ha

w.s.

Hb

Stay
stitching

r.s.

Hc

w.s.

Pattern pieces

There are 32 pattern pieces for Hermione's whole outfit, numbered H1 to H32 and printed on pages 109-119.

The tailored self-lined bodice has elbow-length sleeves and a braided cape collar, half cuffs and small peplum. A self-lined braided overskirt with a bustle effect is attached to the bodice waist. There is a lace jabot (page 99) at the neck.

Materials and notions

1m (39in) taffeta 115cm (45in) wide
3.30m (130in) Russia braid
Four buttons
Two ribbon rosettes
24cm (9½in) cotton lace 2.5cm (1in) wide
70cm (27½in) cotton lace 1cm (½in) wide
Sewing thread to match

Pattern pieces There are five pattern pieces for the bodice, numbered H1 to H5, and three pattern pieces for the overskirt, numbered H6 to H8.
Note: Mark braid placement lines on the fabric using dressmaker's carbon paper.

Making instructions

1 (Ha) With r.s.f., stitch the cape collar to the cape collar lining around the outside edge leaving the neck and front edges open.
2 Clip the seam, turn to the r.s. and press.
3 With the r.s. of the collar uppermost, sew Russia braid along the lines indicated on the pattern.
4 With r.s.f., stitch the peplum to the peplum lining round the outer edge leaving the waist edge open.
5 Clip the seam, turn to the right side and press.
6 Stitch Russia braid on the right side of the peplum as indicated on the pattern.
7 On the lining side of the cuff sew a row of Russia braid as marked on the pattern. This will turn back to form the r.s. on the finished garment.
8 With r.s.f., seam the sleeve to the sleeve lining across the wrist edge.
9 Repeat Instructions 7 and 8 for the other sleeve.
10 Stitch all darts on the bodice back, bodice fronts and lining pieces and press towards the side seams.
11 With r.s.f., stitch shoulder seams on bodice.
12 Repeat with the lining.
13 (Hb) Stay stitch up one front, around the neck and back down the other front.
14 Repeat with the lining.
15 With the lining side of the collar facing the r.s. of the bodice, and matching notches, tack the collar in place.
16 (Hc) With r.s.f. and enclosing the collar, sew the bodice lining to the bodice, up one front, around the neckline, and back down the other front.
17 Gather each bodice sleeve head and each lining sleeve head individually, between the gathering lines.
18 With r.s.f., stitch the bodice sleeve head to the bodice armhole.
19 Repeat with the second sleeve.
20 (Hd) Matching armhole seams and with r.s.f., stitch bodice side seam, stitch across armhole seam and down sleeve seam, taking care to fold cuff in place before stitching, continue up sleeve lining. Do not sew bodice lining at this stage.

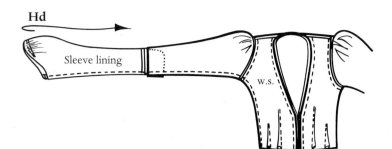

Hd

Sleeve lining

w.s.

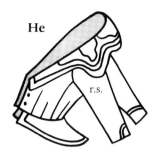

He

r.s.

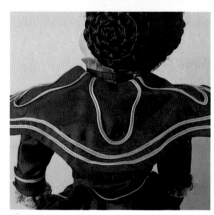

21 Repeat with the other side.

22 With r.s.f., seam together the lining side seams.

23 Press seams open and turn to the right side.

24 (He) Matching notches, attach the r.s. of the peplum to the r.s. of the bodice leaving the lining free.

25 Mark the decorative braid design on the right side of the overskirt using dressmaker's carbon paper.

26 With r.s.f., seam overskirt to overskirt lining, leaving waist edge open.

27 Clip seams, press and turn to the r.s.

28 Sew the Russia braid on the marked line through all layers.

29 (Hf) Pleat sides as indicated on the pattern (the pleats face upwards on the right side) and top stitch in place.

30 Run two rows of gathering between Xs on pattern and pull up to measure 8cm (3in). Top stitch over the gathers.

31 Sew a ribbon rosette on each X.

32 Gather the waist of the overskirt and pull up to fit between the notches on the bodice.

33 (Hg) Sew the overskirt to the waist edge of the bodice. Turn bodice lining under and hand stitch in place at waist.

34 Turn under armhole edge of bodice lining and hand stitch to the armhole. Repeat with the other armhole.

35 Sew a row of machine stitching on the bodice around the neck, directly beneath the cape collar, through all layers.

36 Sew two buttons to the left front and make sewn loops (see page 14) to correspond on the right front. Optional: sew two additional buttons to the right front to make the jacket double-breasted. Decorative buttons may be sewn to the sleeve cuffs.

37 (Hh) Cut a 12cm (4¾in) length of wide lace, and a 35cm (14in) length of narrow lace. Gather the narrow lace and sew two rows, one above the other, on the right side of the wide lace. Gather the top of the wide lace and hand sew it round the bottom of the bodice sleeve.

38 Repeat for the other sleeve.

Hf

r.s.

Hg

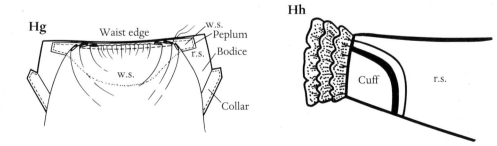

Waist edge

w.s. Peplum

r.s. Bodice

w.s.

Collar

Hh

Cuff

r.s.

Skirt ★★

The skirt is self lined and has a train with a flounce at the hemline. Small beads are sewn to a row of gathered lace just above the flounce. The skirt has a centre back opening.

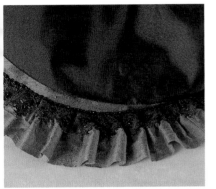

Materials and notions

1m (39in) silk 115cm (45in) wide
1.5m (59in) cotton lace 2.5cm (1in) wide
One hook and eye
Small beads
Sewing thread to match

Pattern pieces

There are six pattern pieces for the skirt, numbered H9 to H14.

Making instructions

1 Sew the darts on the front and back skirt pieces and press towards the skirt sides.
2 Repeat with the skirt lining.
3 With r.s.f. sew the centre back seam of the skirt leaving a small opening at the waist.
4 Repeat with the skirt lining.
5 With r.s.f., sew skirt side seams and press open.
6 Repeat with the skirt lining.
7 (Hi) Join skirt frill to form a circle and press in half lengthwise with w.s.f.
8 (Hi) Stitch two rows of gathering stitches through both layers along the top of the frill and pull up to fit the skirt hem.
9 R.s.f. and raw edges level stitch the frill to the skirt hem.
10 With r.s.f., and enclosing the frill, sew the lining to the skirt around the hem.
11 Clip seam, press and turn to the right side.
12 (Hj) Neaten the back opening by turning the raw edges to the inside and stitching around the opening.
13 Run two rows of gathering stitches around the waist between the notches. Keeping the front of the skirt flat, pull up the gathers so that the waist measures 20cm (8in).
14 With r.s.f., sew the waistband in place through all layers.
15 Fold the waistband over, turn under a narrow hem and hand sew to the lining.
16 Sew a hook and eye to fasten the waistband.
17 Optional: stitch a row of gathered lace to the hem just above the flounce, and decorate the lace with small beads.

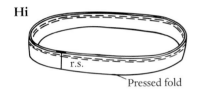

Hi

r.s.

Pressed fold

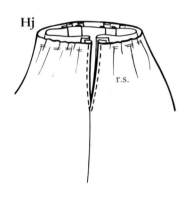

Hj

r.s.

Lace jabot & neckband ★★

The lace jabot is horseshoe in shape and is attached to a pleated neckband. It is decorated with loops of small beads, and there is a brooch in the centre of the neckband.

Materials and notions

41cm (16in) cotton lace 2.5cm (1in) wide
1m (39in) cotton lace 1cm (½in) wide
33cm (13in) silk 6cm (2½in) wide – there is sufficient fabric in the amount given for the skirt (above)
17cm (6½in) taffeta 1.5cm (½in) wide – there is sufficient fabric in the amount given for the bodice (page 96)
Small beads

Hk

r.s.

Step 8
Step 7
Step 6
Step 3
Step 4
Step 1
Step 2

Hl

Hm

Hn

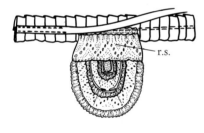

r.s.

Sewing thread to match

A small brooch (optional) – an earring or button is often the right size to use as a brooch

Pattern pieces There are two pattern pieces for the jabot and neckband, numbered H15 and H16. The finished shape on page 116 is a guide for assembling the jabot.

Making instructions

1 (Hk) Using 15cm (6in) of wide lace, make two small pleats in the middle to form a horseshoe shape.

2 (Hk) Sew a row of gathered narrow lace to the top and bottom edge of the shape.

3 (Hk) Using 11cm (4½in) of wide lace repeat Instruction 1.

4 (Hk) Sew a length of gathered narrow lace around the inside of the smaller horseshoe.

5 (Hk) Sew the second smaller horseshoe to lie inside the larger horseshoe.

6 (Hk) Sew a small scrap of lace to fill the centre of the smaller horseshoe.

7 (Hk) Cut an 8cm (3in) length of wide lace and sew the bottom edge of the lace across the top of the horseshoes.

8 (Hk) Hand sew a length of gathered narrow lace along the top and pull up the stitches to gather the top.

9 Neaten the long edges on the jabot neckband and press them inwards so that they just overlap in the middle.

10 (Hl) Stitch down the middle to hold the hems in place.

11 (Hm) Pleat the neckband to fit the doll's neck, sewing a second row of stitching down the middle to hold the pleats in place.

12 (Hn) Tack the lace jabot in the centre of the neckband, w.s. of lace to r.s.of neckband.

13 (Hn) Cover the two rows of stitching by sewing a row of narrow ribbon or a strip of contrasting fabric down the middle of the neckband, on top of the stitching, catching the top edge of the lace jabot.

14 Sew a hook and eye on the ends of the neckband.

15 Small beads have been hung in loops from the neckband and a small brooch has been pinned to the centre (see top photo, page 98).

Hat★★★

The hat has a small crown and is worn on the front of the head. It has a narrow turned-up brim and is extravagantly trimmed with feathers, flowers, ribbon loops and velvet leaves.

Materials and notions

38cm (15in) taffeta 13cm (5in) wide – there is sufficient fabric in the amount given for the bodice (page 96).

25cm (10in) buckram 13cm (5in) wide

40cm (16in) silk 4cm (1½in) wide cut on the bias – cut this from the skirt fabric (page 99)

Millinery wire, or fine florists' wire

A hatpin

Trimmings: feathers, assorted ribbons for making ribbon loops, flowers and leaves

Optional: a circle of taffeta about the size of a saucer, and a length of gathered and beaded lace to fit around half the circle

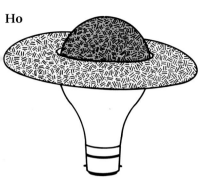

Ho

Hp

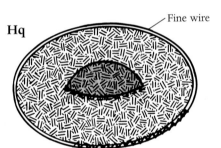

Hq

Fine wire

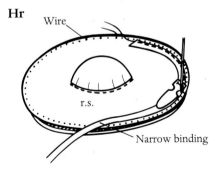

Hr

Wire

r.s.

Narrow binding

Pattern pieces

There are four pattern pieces for the hat, numbered H17 to H20.

Making instructions

1 Snip round the buckram crown as indicated on the pattern piece.
2 Dampen the buckram crown and mould over a round object the same size as the doll's head – an electric light bulb, for example (not connected!)
3 (Ho) Slip the brim over the crown and bend the crown edges outwards so that they lie against the underside of the brim.
4 (Hp) Allow to dry. This can be speeded up with a hair dryer.
5 Tack brim to crown.
6 (Hq) Sew millinery wire around the edge of the brim. You could use fine florists' wire.
7 Gather the crown fabric around the edge, and pull up the gathers evenly so that the crown fabric fits over the buckram shape.
8 Tack the crown in place on the buckram shape.
9 Neaten the inside edge of the brim fabric using a small closed-up zigzag stitch.
10 Pull the brim fabric over the crown and stitch in place. Straight stitch on the sewing machine sewn with the zip foot is satisfactory, but you may prefer to sew the hat by hand.
11 Gather the crown lining around the edge. Pull up to fit inside edge of brim.
12 Repeat Instruction 9 with the brim lining.
13 With the w.s. of the brim lining against the r.s. of the crown lining and using the zip foot, straight stitch the crown lining to the brim lining.
14 Insert the lining into the inside of the buckram hat shape.
15 Using the zip foot and straight stitch sew close to the wire, around the outer edge of the hat brim, through all layers.
16 (Hr) R.s.f., and again using the zip foot, sew the binding to the right side of the hat brim, this time sewing inside the wire edge.
17 Turn the binding to the underside of the brim, turn under the raw edge and hand stitch to the brim lining.
18 Sew a narrow braid or ribbon where the crown meets the brim. Trim the hat to suit your doll using feathers, ribbons, leaves and flowers.
19 Optional decoration: with r.s.f. and the gathered edge of the lace level with the raw edge of the circle, sew the lace around half of the circle.
20 Fold the circle of taffeta in half, r.s.f., and sew together around the edge on the same stitching line leaving a small opening for turning.
21 Clip seam, turn to the r.s. and press. Close the opening with hand stitching.
22 Gather the straight edge of the semi-circle and pull up to form a fan shape, sew between the feathers and leaves on the hat.
23 Bend the brim to suit your doll's face. Hold the hat in place with a small hat pin.

Bustle pad★

This is tied around the waist to extend the fullness at the back of the skirt. Princess Marie Louise, Napoleon I's first wife, once described the bustle as an exaggerated pin cushion!

Materials and notions

30cm (12in) fabric 10cm (4in) wide – there is sufficient fabric in the amount given for the pantaloons (page 102)
50cm (20in) narrow tape or ribbon
Small amount of stuffing

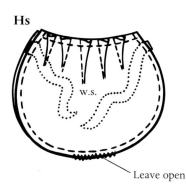

Hs

Leave open

w.s.

Pattern pieces There is one pattern piece for the bustle pad, numbered H21 (page 109).

Making instructions

1 Sew the darts on the bustle, and press towards the side seams.
2 Repeat with the bustle lining.
3 Sew narrow ribbon or tape ties to the bustle – see notches on the pattern for placement.
4 (Hs) With r.s.f., seam bustle to bustle lining leaving a small opening at the bottom for turning. Take care not to trap the ties in the seam.
5 Clip seams, turn bustle to the r.s. and press.
6 Stuff the bustle and close the opening with hand stitching.

Waist petticoat★

The petticoat is on a waistband with a centre back opening. It has a train with a double row of lace around the hem. If made in a stiff fabric, it will hold the skirt out.

Materials and notions
50cm (20in) stiff satin 115cm (45in) wide
115cm (45in) cotton lace 1.5cm (¾in)wide
115cm (45in) cotton scalloped edging 1.5cm (¾in) wide
One hook and eye
Sewing thread to match

Pattern pieces Use the four pattern pieces numbered H9 to H12 (skirt pattern).

Making instructions

1 Sew all darts on the petticoat front and back and press towards the side seams. Neaten all edges except the waist edge.
2 R.s.f., seam up the side seams, and press seams open.
3 R.s.f., sew back seam leaving a small opening at the waist and press open. Turn a narrow hem to the inside at the centre back waist opening. Stitch in place.
4 Turn up a single hem round the bottom edge.
5 Sew a row of scalloped lace to the back of the hem.
6 Sew a row of lace on the r.s. of the petticoat just above the hem line.
7 Gather the waist of the petticoat between the notches and pull up to fit the waistband.
8 With r.s.f., sew the waistband to the petticoat. Fold the waistband over to the w.s., turn under a narrow hem and hand stitch in place.
9 Sew a hook and eye to the ends of the waistband.

Pantaloons★★

The pantaloons are made from finest silk. They have a centre back opening, and a length of tape or ribbon is threaded through the waistband to draw them up to fit. The legs have lace-edged tucks at the ankles.

Materials and notions
28cm (11in) fine silk 115cm (45in) wide – this is also sufficient for the chemisette
1m (39in) narrow cotton lace
50cm (20in) narrow tape or ribbon
Sewing thread to match

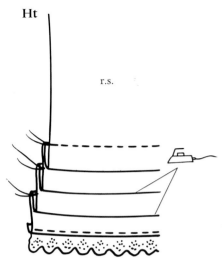

Ht

r.s.

Pattern pieces There are two pattern pieces for the pantaloons, numbered H22 and H23.

Making instructions

1 Neaten all edges.
2 Turn up and stitch a single hem at the bottom of the leg. Sew a row of flat lace to the bottom of the hem on the w.s.
3 (Ht) Press tucks in place and stitch the three bottom tucks.
4 Stitch a row of lace to the back of each bottom tuck; the edge of the lace should protrude below the tuck(s).
5 (Hu) Stitch a row of ribbon or wider lace along the top of the row of tucks.
6 Stitch the top tuck above the row of lace.
7 R.s.f. and starting at the ankle edge seam up the inside leg seam.
8 Repeat Instructions 2-7 with the other leg.
9 R.s.f., seam round the crotch between the notches.
10 Turn a small hem to the w.s. around the back opening and stitch in place.
11 Pin the two unpressed pleats on the front of the pantaloons.
12 R.s.f., stitch the waistband to the waist, fold over to the w.s., turn under a narrow hem and slip stitch in place by hand leaving the ends open.
13 (Hv) Thread narrow ribbon or tape through the waistband.

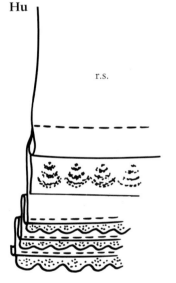

Hu

r.s.

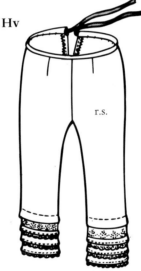

Hv

r.s.

Chemisette★

The chemisette is self lined and is front fastening. It has rows of lace, ribbon and tiny seed pearls decorating the front. The waist has a drawstring and the hem is scalloped.

Materials and notions
20cm (8in) fine silk 115cm (45in) wide – there is sufficient fabric for the chemisette in the amount given for the pantaloons (opposite)
30cm (12in) cotton lace 3cm (1in) wide
1m (39in) narrow satin ribbon
Small pearls for decoration
Three small hooks and eyes

Pattern pieces There are two pattern pieces for the chemisette, numbered H24 and H25.

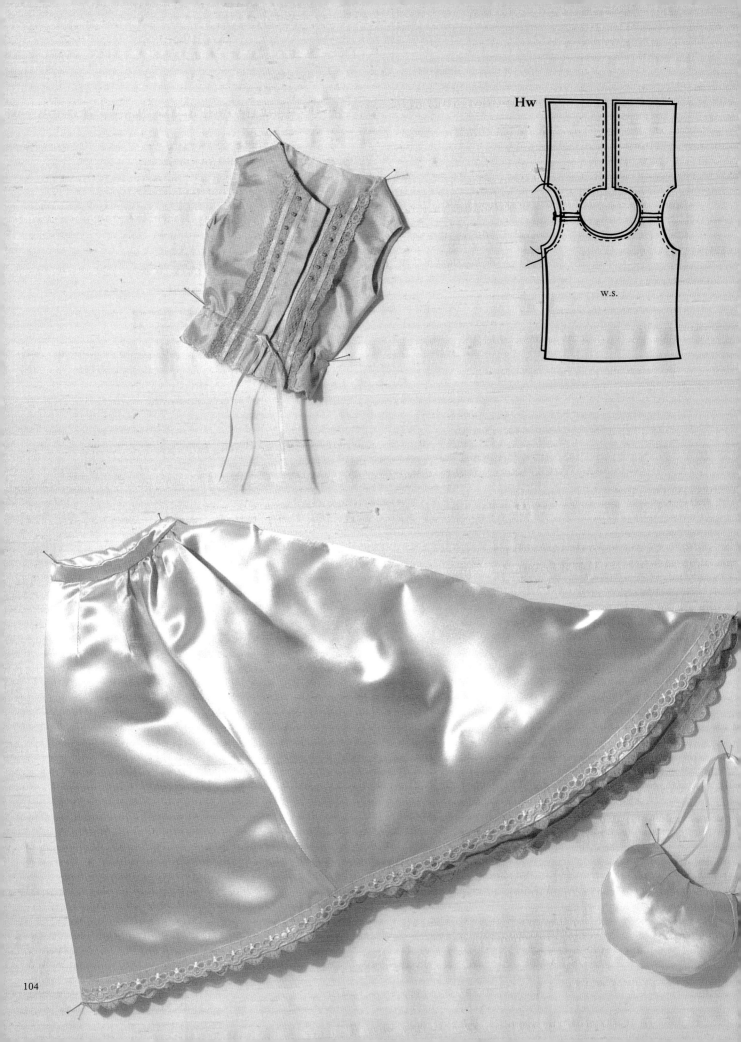

Hw

W.S.

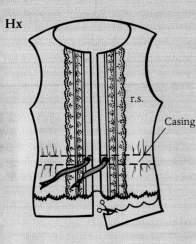

Hx

Making instructions

1. With r.s.f., join the shoulder seams on the chemisette and press them open.
2. Repeat with the lining.
3. Sew rows of ribbon and lace along placement lines on the fronts of the chemisette.
4. Make a small buttonhole on each front as indicated on the pattern.
5. (Hw) R.s.f., sew the chemisette to the lining up the front edge around the neck and down the other front. Press and clip seams.
6. (Hw) Still with the r.s.f., sew the chemisette to the lining around armhole edge. Press and clip seams.
7. Turn to the r.s. by pulling the fronts through the shoulders and press.
8. With r.s.f. and matching armhole seams, sew up the chemisette side seam across the armhole seam and down the lining side seam. Press.
9. Repeat with the other side.
10. (Hx) With the bottom edges level, scallop stitch around the bottom of the chemisette 1cm (⅜in) from the raw edges. Trim the raw edges away. Alternatively, hand sew the scallops using buttonhole stitch.
11. (Hx) Make a casing by sewing two rows of stitching around the waist as indicated on the pattern.
12. (Hx) Thread narrow ribbon into the buttonhole and through the casing.
13. Decorate the fronts with small pearls.
14. Hand sew the hooks and eyes to the front opening.

Lace mittens★

Use stretch lace dyed with fabric paint for the mittens. Sizes of dolls' hands vary, so check that the pattern fits your doll. Stretch lace is easy to handle, but if you wish to be authentic, crochet some lace mittens using the pattern shape as a guide.

Materials and notions
12cm (5in) stretch lace 6cm (2½in) wide

Pattern pieces There is one pattern piece for the mittens, numbered H26.

Making instructions

1. (Hy) Neaten the elbow edge of each mitten by sewing along the edge with a closed up zigzag stitch.

2 (Hz) Using the same stitch, and with r.s.f., sew up the inner arm seam.

3 Trim away the seam allowance close to the stitching line, and turn to the r.s.

4 Repeat with the second mitten.

5 (Haa) Hand stitch the edges together between the thumb and first finger.

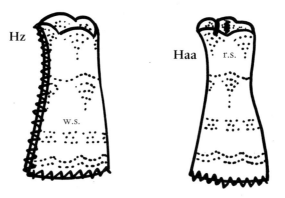

Parasol★

The parasol cover is self lined. It has a frilled lace edging and a buttonhole in the centre to accommodate the stick.

Materials and notions

A parasol stick – if you are unable to buy one, a woodturner who makes lace bobbins may make one for you

41cm (16in) taffeta 21cm (8in) wide – there is sufficient fabric in the amount given for the bodice and overskirt (page 96)

1m (39in) cotton lace, to match the lace on the bottom of the skirt

25cm (10in) narrow satin ribbon

Sewing thread to match

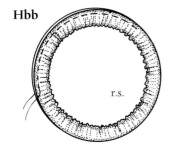

Pattern pieces There is one pattern piece for the parasol, marked H27.

Making instructions

1 Gather the lace to fit the outer edge of the parasol circle.

2 (Hbb) With r.s.f., and the gathered edge of the lace parallel with the outside edge of the parasol circle, stitch the lace in place on the stitching line.

3 With r.s.f., and enclosing the lace, stitch the lining to the parasol around the edge taking care not to catch the free edge of the lace in the seam. Leave an opening to turn the parasol to the r.s.

4 Clip the seam to allow it to form a smooth circle and turn to the r.s. and press.

5 Close the opening with hand stitching.

6 Press the parasol into half then into quarters then into eighths as shown on the pattern piece. Take care not to iron over any creases already pressed.

7 Now turn over the parasol and from the lining side press the same number of creases, but this time they must lie between the creases already pressed.

8 Make a small buttonhole in the centre of the parasol for the stick.

9 Sew the parasol to the bottom of the stick. (If necessary, drill a small hole through the wooden stick.)

10 (Hcc) Run a row of hand stitching catching the top of the inward facing pleats and draw them up so that they fit around the parasol stick.

11 (Hdd) Alternately, the stick can be rotated, flattening the pleats against the stick, where they can be held in place with narrow ribbon.

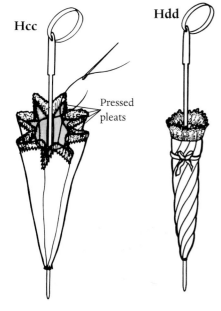

12 Sew a loop of ribbon to the top of the handle.

Socks★★

The socks are hand knitted in cotton. They have a picot edge and lacy side panels.

Materials

One ball No. 8 cotton perlé
One pair 2mm knitting needles
Sewing-up needle

Making instructions

See page 9 for abbreviations.
Cast on 40 sts.

Hem with picot edge
Beginning with a k row knit 4 rows in st.st.
5th row: K1, *k2tog, yf,* repeat from * to * to last st, k1
6th row: P
Knit 4 more rows in st.st.
Commence the pattern
11th row: K5, p2, k2tog, (k1, yf,) twice, k1, sl 1, k1, psso, p2, k8, p2, k2tog, (k1, yf,) twice, k1, sl 1, k1, psso, p2, k5
12th and alt rows: P5, k2, p7, k2, p8, k2, p7, k2, p5
13th row: K5, p2, k2tog, yf, k3, yf, sl 1, k1, psso, p2, k8, p2, k2tog, yf, k3, yf, sl 1, k1, psso, p2, k5
14th row: as 12th
15th row: K5, p2, k1, yf, sl 1, k1, psso, k1, k2tog, yf, k1, p2, k8, p2, k1, yf, sl 1, k1, psso, k1, k2tog, yf, k1, p2, k5
16th row: as 12th
17th row: K5, p2, k2, yf, sl 1, k2tog, psso, yf, k2, p2, k8, p2, k2, yf, sl 1, k2tog, psso, yf, k2, p2, k5
18th row: P5, k2tog, p7, k2tog, p8, k2tog, p7, k2tog, p5, (36 sts)
19th row: K5, p1, k2tog, (k1, yf) twice, k1, sl 1, k1, psso, p1, k8, p1, k2tog, (k1, yf) twice, k1, sl 1, k1, psso, p1, k5
20th and alternate rows: P5, k1, p7, k1, p8, k1, p7, k1, p5
21st row: K5, p1, k2tog, yf, k3, yf, sl 1, k1, psso, p1, k8, p1, k2tog, yf, k3, yf, sl 1, k1, psso, p1, k5
22nd row: as 20th
23rd row: K5, p1, k1, yf, sl 1, k1, psso k1, k2tog, yf, k1, p1, k8, p1, k1, yf, sl 1, k1, psso, k1, k2tog, yf, k1, p1, k5
24th row: as 20th
25th row: K5, p1, k2, yf, sl 1, k2tog, psso, yf, k2, p1, k8, p1, k2, yf, sl 1, k2tog, psso, yf, k2, p1, k5
26th row: as 20th

Foot shaping
27th row: K13, p1, k8, p1, turn
28th row: K1, p8, k1, turn
Keeping the pattern correct continue knitting on the 10 centre sts for a further 8 rows
37th row: P1, k8, p1 [the 10 centre sts], pick up and k 6 sts along the side edge of the centre front, k across the 13 sts left on the needle (29 sts)
38th row: P19, k1, p8, k1, pick up 6 sts, along the side edge of the centre front and p the remaining 13 sts (48 sts)

39th row: K19, p1, k8, p1, k19
40th row: P19, k1, p8, k1, p19
41st to 44th rows: repeat the last 2 rows twice

Heel shaping
45th row: K2tog k17, p1, sl 1, k1, psso, k4, k2tog, p1, k17, k2tog
46th row: P2tog, p16, k1 sl 1, p1, psso, p2, p2tog, k1, p16, p2tog
47th row: K2tog, k15, p1, sl 1, k1, psso, k2tog, p1, k15, k2tog
48th row: P2tog, p14, k1, p2tog, k1, p14, p2tog (33 sts)
Cast off

Seam along the bottom of the sole and up the back of the leg.
Turn over a small hem at the top of the sock and slip stitch in place.
Repeat the instructions for the other sock.

Boots*

The boots are made from fine soft leather, and machine stitched. The leather may need a backing to pass easily under the machine foot. Use a strip of till roll or stitch-and-tear Vilene, and tear the backing off after stitching. Tiny beads are sewn to the sides of the boots as buttons. Optional: cut a small design from soft leather in a contrasting colour and stick as decoration on to the front of each boot.

Materials and notions
20cm (8in) soft leather 12cm (5in) wide
Six small beads
Glue (contact adhesive)
Sewing thread to match
Cardboard for the boot insoles, picture mounting quality
Thin cardboard for the sole infills
A leather punch
Small piece of contrast leather for decoration (optional)

Pattern pieces There are five pattern pieces for the boots, numbered H28 to H32.

Making instructions
1 Stick boot toe cap to boot leg, matching symbols.
2 (Hee) Stitch around the top and side edges of the leather as indicated on the pattern piece, and across the toe cap.
3 Overlap the leg of the boot and stitch one-third of the way up the leg starting at the sole edge.
4 Put a layer of glue around the shaded edge of the cardboard sole as shown on the pattern.
5 Put the boot on the doll's foot and, using the foot as a last, place the cardboard sole (glue side facing outwards) on to the doll's foot. Pull the leather down and bend it smoothly round so that it sticks onto the glued edge of the cardboard.
6 Cut a thin card infill the size of the non-shaded area on the insole pattern and stick to the cardboard sole between the edges of the leather upper.
7 Glue the leather sole and heel in place.
8 Punch buttonholes down the side of the boot leg as indicated in the pattern.
9 Sew small beads as buttons to correspond with the buttonholes.
10 Repeat Instructions 1-9 with the other boot.
11 Optional: cut two small designs from the contrast leather and glue one to the front of each boot.

Hee

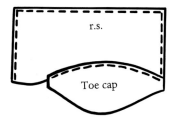

r.s.

Toe cap

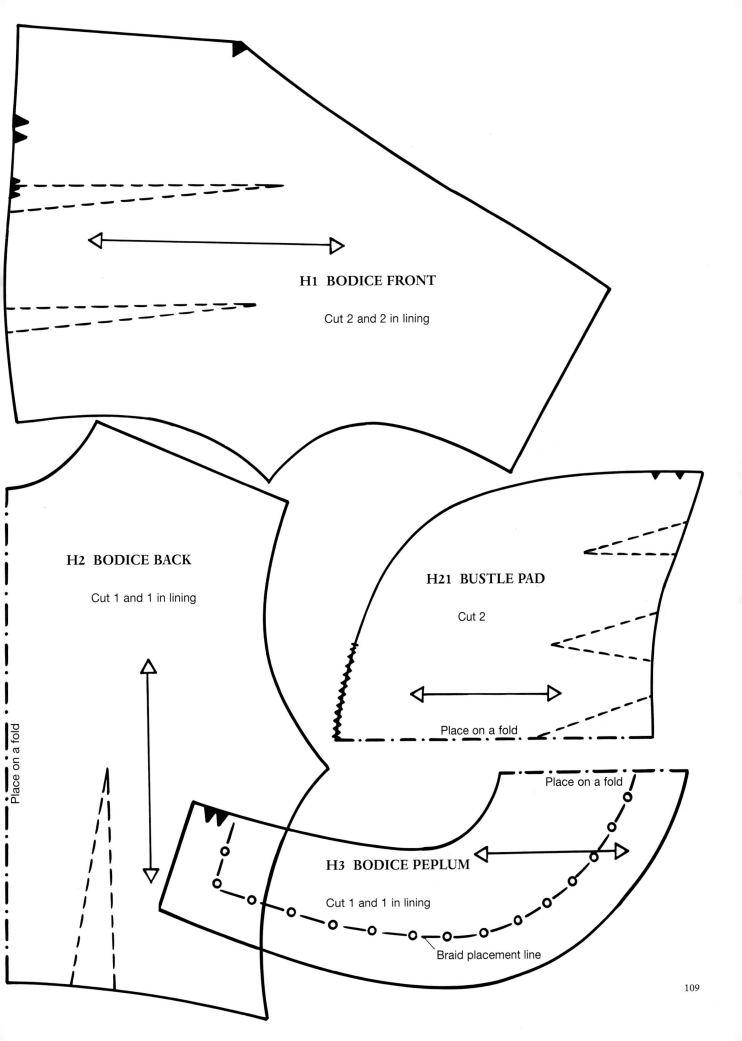

H1 BODICE FRONT

Cut 2 and 2 in lining

H2 BODICE BACK

Cut 1 and 1 in lining

Place on a fold

H21 BUSTLE PAD

Cut 2

Place on a fold

Place on a fold

H3 BODICE PEPLUM

Cut 1 and 1 in lining

Braid placement line

109

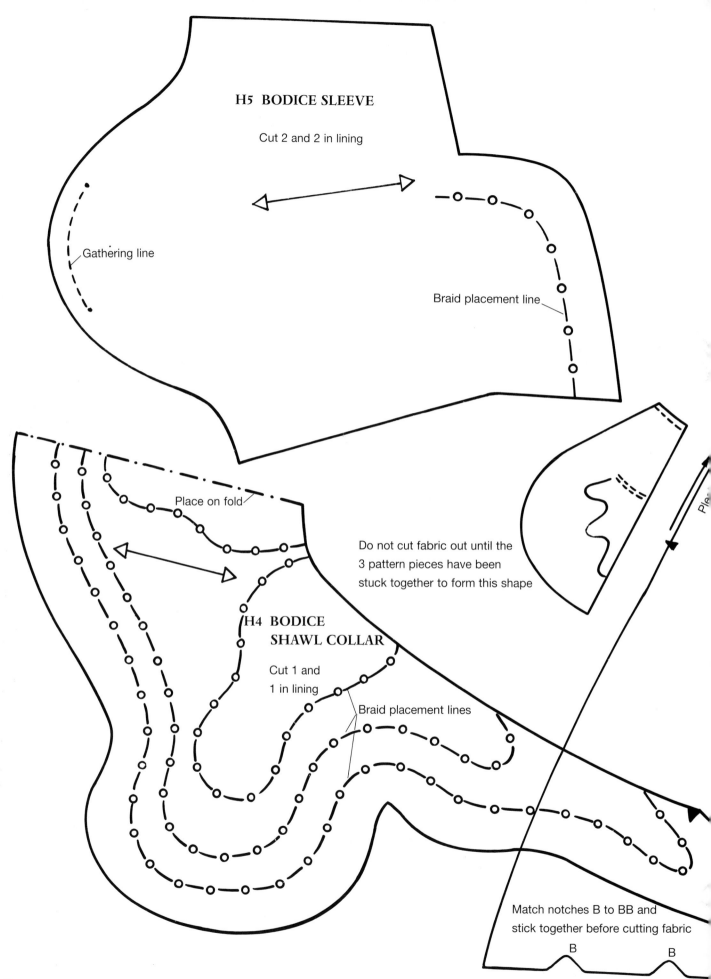

H5 BODICE SLEEVE

Cut 2 and 2 in lining

Gathering line

Braid placement line

Place on fold

Do not cut fabric out until the
3 pattern pieces have been
stuck together to form this shape

**H4 BODICE
SHAWL COLLAR**

Cut 1 and
1 in lining

Braid placement lines

Match notches B to BB and
stick together before cutting fabric

B   B

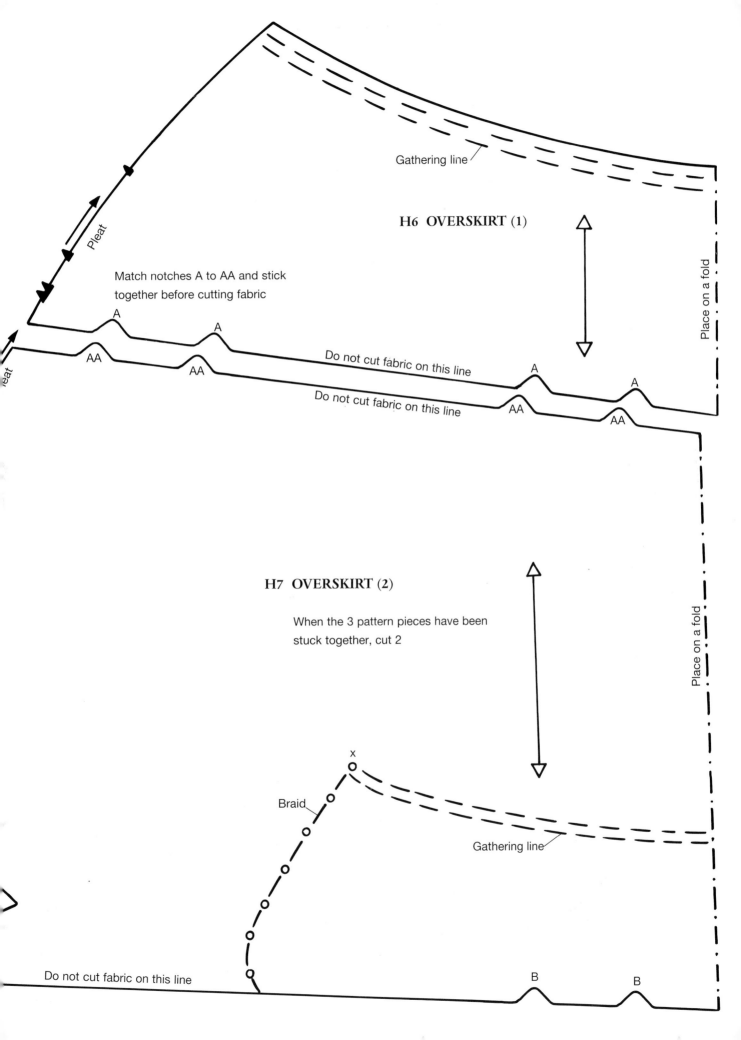

Gathering line

H6 OVERSKIRT (1)

Pleat

Match notches A to AA and stick
together before cutting fabric

A

AA

A

AA

Do not cut fabric on this line

A

AA

A

AA

Do not cut fabric on this line

Pleat

Place on a fold

H7 OVERSKIRT (2)

When the 3 pattern pieces have been
stuck together, cut 2

Place on a fold

X

Braid

Gathering line

Do not cut fabric on this line

B

B

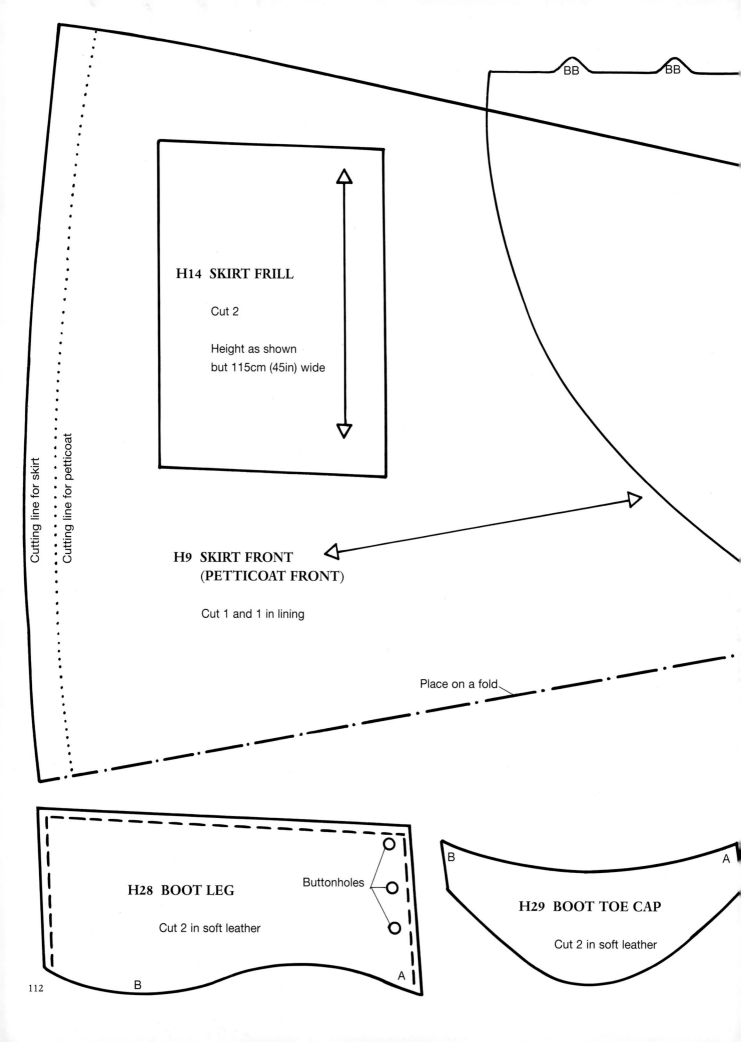

BB   BB

H14 SKIRT FRILL

Cut 2

Height as shown
but 115cm (45in) wide

Cutting line for skirt

Cutting line for petticoat

**H9 SKIRT FRONT
(PETTICOAT FRONT)**

Cut 1 and 1 in lining

Place on a fold

H28 BOOT LEG

Cut 2 in soft leather

Buttonholes

B

A

B   A

H29 BOOT TOE CAP

Cut 2 in soft leather

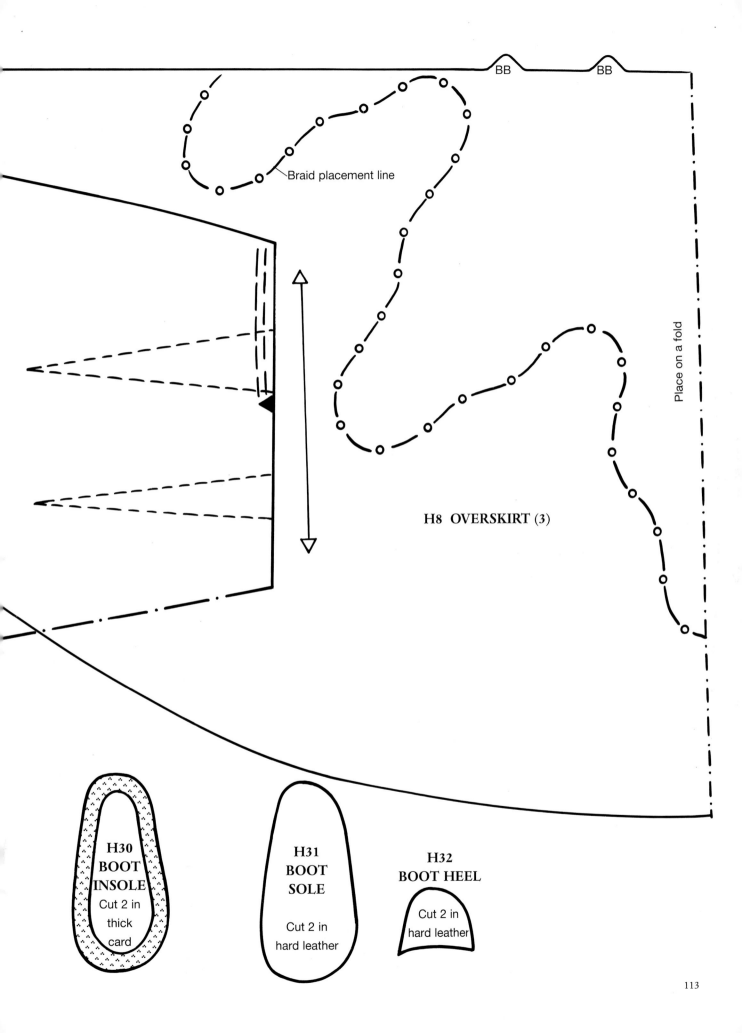

BB   BB

Braid placement line

Place on a fold

H8 OVERSKIRT (3)

**H30
BOOT
INSOLE**
Cut 2 in
thick
card

**H31
BOOT
SOLE**

Cut 2 in
hard leather

**H32
BOOT HEEL**

Cut 2 in
hard leather

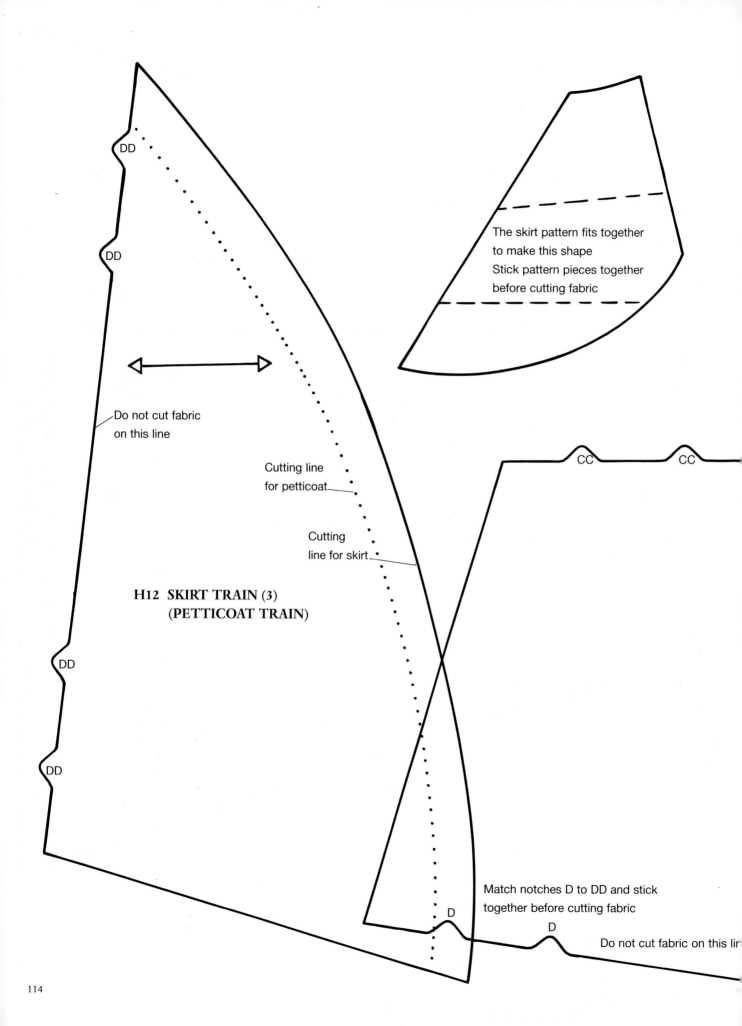

DD

DD

The skirt pattern fits together
to make this shape
Stick pattern pieces together
before cutting fabric

Do not cut fabric
on this line

Cutting line
for petticoat

CC   CC

Cutting
line for skirt

**H12 SKIRT TRAIN (3)
(PETTICOAT TRAIN)**

DD

DD

Match notches D to DD and stick
together before cutting fabric

D

D

Do not cut fabric on this lir

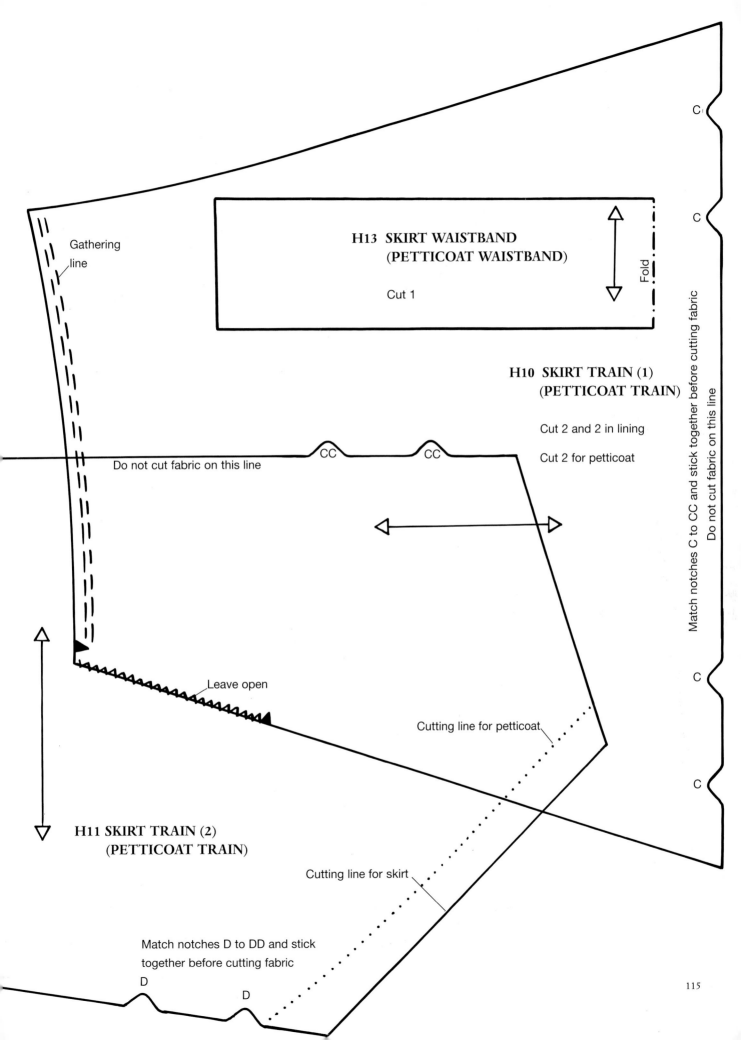

H13 SKIRT WAISTBAND
(PETTICOAT WAISTBAND)

Fold

Cut 1

Gathering line

H10 SKIRT TRAIN (1)
(PETTICOAT TRAIN)

Cut 2 and 2 in lining

Cut 2 for petticoat

Do not cut fabric on this line

CC   CC

C

C

Match notches C to CC and stick together before cutting fabric

Do not cut fabric on this line

C

C

Leave open

Cutting line for petticoat

H11 SKIRT TRAIN (2)
(PETTICOAT TRAIN)

Cutting line for skirt

Match notches D to DD and stick together before cutting fabric

D   D

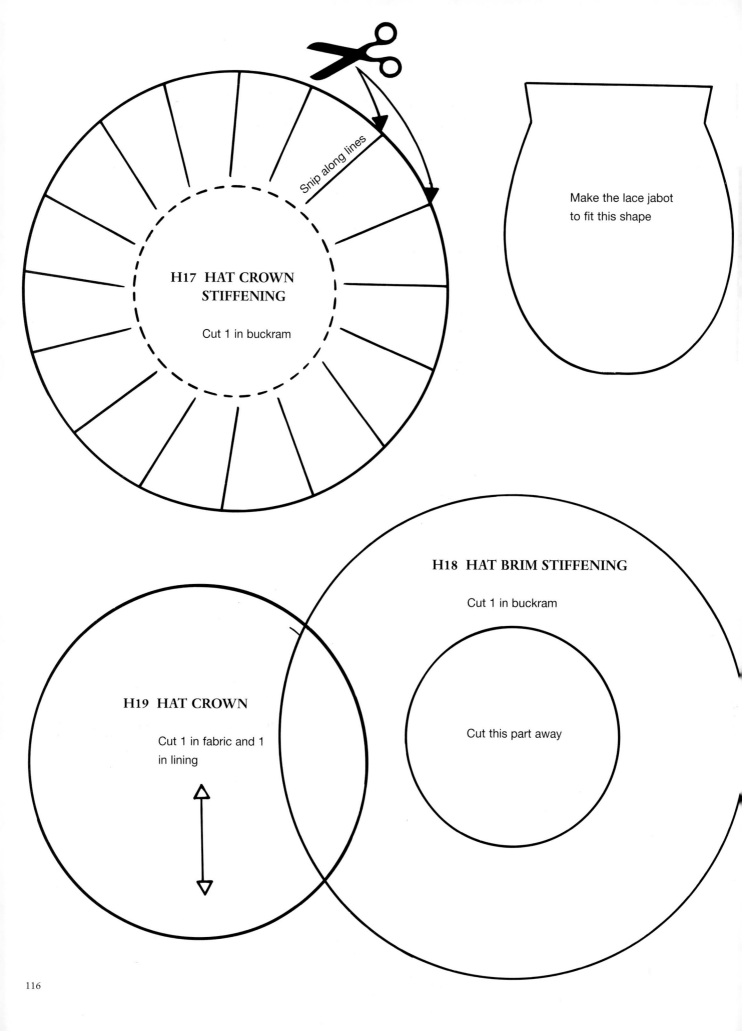

H17 HAT CROWN STIFFENING

Cut 1 in buckram

Snip along lines

Make the lace jabot to fit this shape

H18 HAT BRIM STIFFENING

Cut 1 in buckram

Cut this part away

H19 HAT CROWN

Cut 1 in fabric and 1 in lining

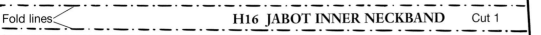

Fold lines **H16 JABOT INNER NECKBAND** Cut 1

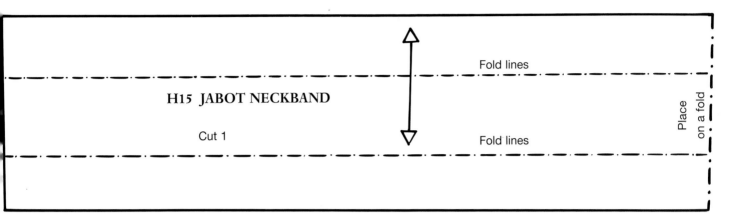

Fold lines

H15 JABOT NECKBAND

Cut 1

Fold lines

Place on a fold

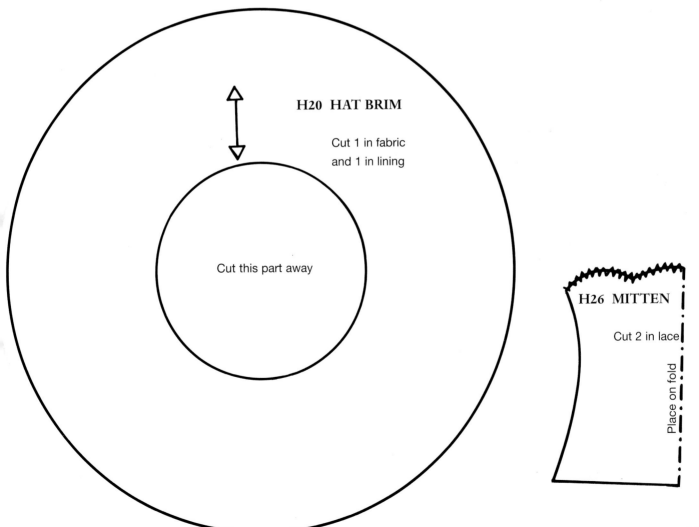

H20 HAT BRIM

Cut 1 in fabric
and 1 in lining

Cut this part away

H26 MITTEN

Cut 2 in lace

Place on fold

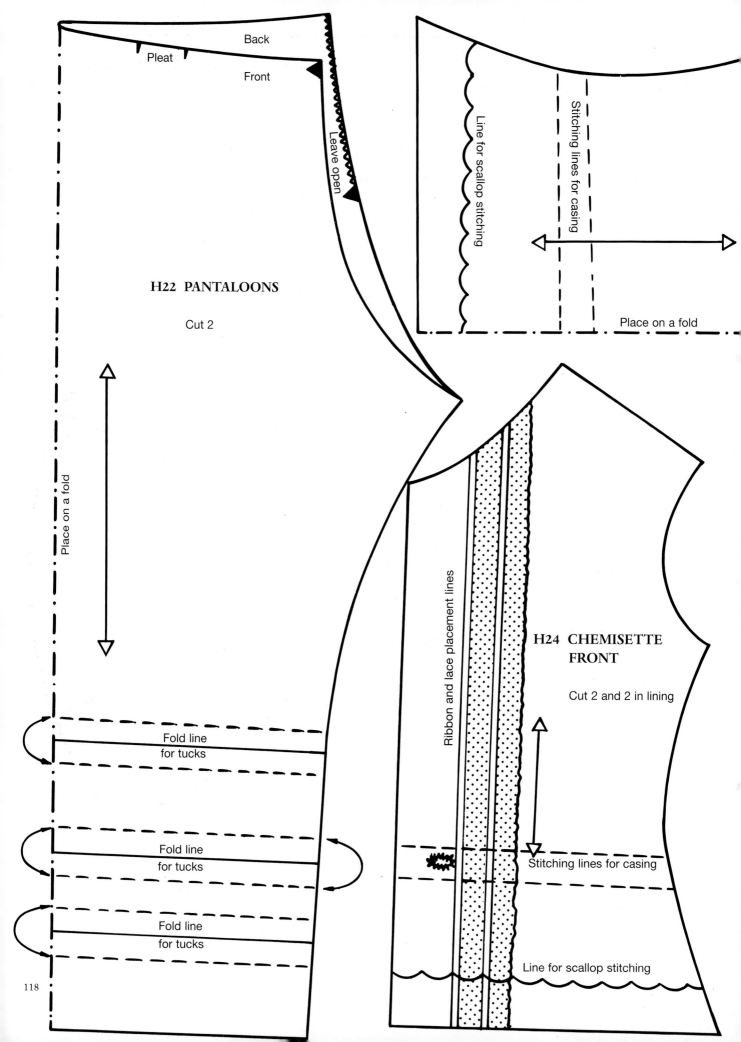

Back

Pleat

Front

Leave open

H22 PANTALOONS

Cut 2

Place on a fold

Fold line
for tucks

Fold line
for tucks

Fold line
for tucks

Line for scallop stitching

Stitching lines for casing

Place on a fold

Ribbon and lace placement lines

H24 CHEMISETTE FRONT

Cut 2 and 2 in lining

Stitching lines for casing

Line for scallop stitching

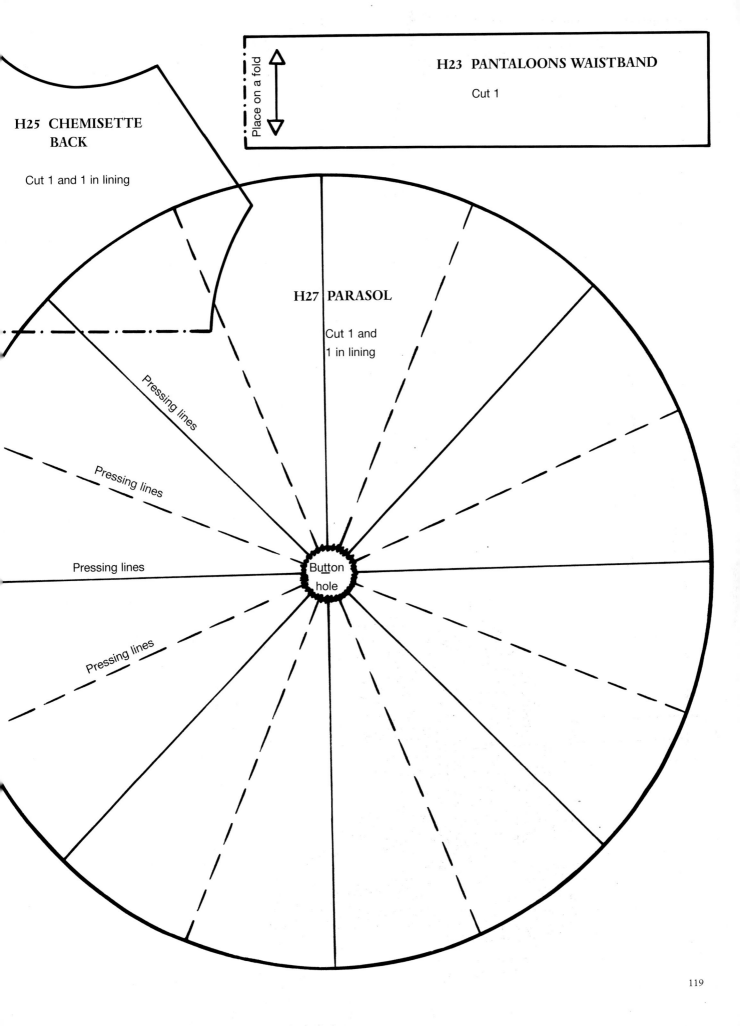

H25 CHEMISETTE BACK

Cut 1 and 1 in lining

Place on a fold

H23 PANTALOONS WAISTBAND

Cut 1

H27 PARASOL

Cut 1 and 1 in lining

Pressing lines

Pressing lines

Pressing lines

Pressing lines

Button hole

119

BERNADETTE

Travelling ensemble

The doll pictured is a reproduction from an antique doll produced by the Jumeau factory in Paris and is marked 'E14J'. She has a porcelain head on a composition body, pierced ears, glass paperweight eyes and her wig is made of mohair. Bernadette's outfit consists of a fitted jacket, picture hat, dress, waist petticoat, bloomers, camisole, socks, leather-fringed boots and bag. The jacket, hat, dress, waist petticoat, camisole and drawers are lined.

Dimensions

Height: 48cm (19in)

Circumference of head: 30cm (11¾in)

Waist: 24cm (9½in)

Neck: 15cm (6in)

Pattern pieces There are 39 pattern pieces for Bernadette's entire outfit, numbered B1 to B39 and printed on pages 134-143.

Jacket★★

The stylish, fitted velvet jacket is waist length at the front and has a deep curved peplum at the back. The sleeves are full and gathered. The revers, cuffs, lower pleated detail, back bow and lining are made from taffeta in a contrasting colour.

Ba

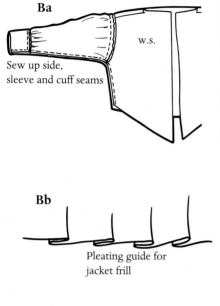

Sew up side, sleeve and cuff seams

w.s.

Materials and notions
20cm (8in) velvet 115cm (45in) wide
45cm (18in) taffeta 115cm (45in) wide
Two buttons or frogs
Thread to match

Pattern pieces There are eight pattern pieces for the jacket, numbered B1 to B8.

Making instructions

1 With r.s.f., seam the shoulder seams, press. Repeat with the lining.
2 Gather the bottom of the sleeve between notches and pull up to fit the cuff. With r.s.f., sew sleeve to cuff. Repeat with the second sleeve.
3 Gather the sleeve heading between the notches and ease the gathers to fit the armhole. With r.s.f., sew sleeve to armhole. Repeat with the second sleeve and the lining.
4 (Ba) R.s.f., sew up side seams, matching armhole seams and continue down the sleeves and cuffs, press. Repeat with the lining, omitting the cuff seam.
5 (Bb) With w.s.f., press the strip of taffeta to be pleated in half lengthways. Sew along the raw edge through both layers making small pleats, as shown on the pleating guide, as you go. Press. Repeat with the other strip.
6 (Bc) R.s.f., and raw edges level, sew the pleats around the bottom curved edge of the peplum. Cut off the excess pleating.
7 With r.s.f., raw edges level, and enclosing the pleats, sew the peplum to the lining around the bottom curved edge. Clip the seam, turn to the r.s. and press.
8 R.s.f., and taking care not to catch the lining, sew the peplum to the back waist edge of the jacket between side seams.
9 With r.s.f., sew lining to jacket up one front, around the neck and down the other front. Clip seams. Do not turn.
10 (Bd) With r.s.f., and taking care not to catch the lining, sew a length of pleated taffeta along the waist edge of each front.
11 With r.s.f. and enclosing the pleats, stitch the front to the lining along the bottom edge on the same line of stitching. Repeat with the other side, clip seams, turn to the r.s. and press.
12 Turn a narrow hem to the w.s. of the jacket back lining at the waist and hand stitch to the peplum.
13 (Be) Sew a button on the bottom of each front, make a stitched loop to fasten. Alternatively, sew frogs to fasten the fronts.
14 Fold the bow in half lengthways and, with r.s.f. and raw edges level, sew around the edge leaving an opening for turning. Clip seam and turn to the r.s.. Press.

Bb

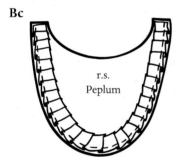

Pleating guide for jacket frill

Bc

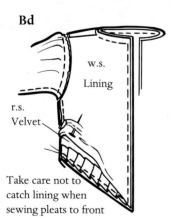

r.s.
Peplum

Bd

w.s.
Lining

r.s.
Velvet

Take care not to catch lining when sewing pleats to front

Be

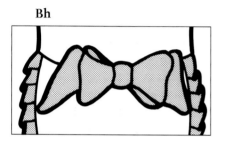

Sew 2 buttons and a stitched button loop to fasten jacket

Bf

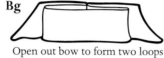

Sew a line of stitching across bow

Bg

Open out bow to form two loops

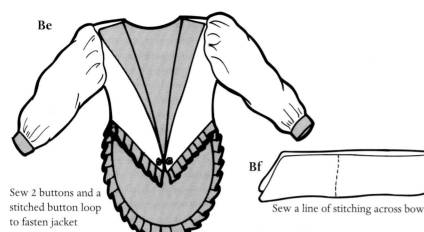

Bh

15 (Bf; Bg) Fold the bow in half and sew a line of stitching across the bow as indicated on the pattern. Open out to make two loops and wind the bow knot around the centre of the bow.

16 (Bh) Hand stitch the bow knot at the back and sew the bow to the centre of the jacket back on the waistline.

Picture hat ★★

The ornate hat has a large wired brim which is extravagantly ruched and trimmed with a profusion of flowers, feathers and wide taffeta loops.

Materials and notions

25cm (10in) velvet 115cm (45in) wide for the crown and top of the brim
25cm (10in) buckram 60cm (24in) wide for the hat base
45cm (18in) taffeta 115cm (45in) wide for the hat lining, gathered brim and loops
70cm (28in) length of millinery wire
Flowers
Feathers
Sewing thread to match
A hatpin

Pattern pieces There are four pattern pieces for the hat, numbered B9 to B12.

Making instructions

1 Overlap the short edges of the buckram crown and seam together to form a tube.

2 (Bi) Snip the edges of the circular buckram crown top. Dampen these edges and bend them downwards to fit inside the top of the crown tube. It is helpful to place this on the top of a round tin which is of a similar size. Leave until dry and set in shape.

3 Snip the inside edges of the buckram brim, dampen these edges and bend upwards to fit inside the bottom of the crown tube. Again, leave over a tin to dry.

4 (Bj) Place a length of millinery wire around the edge of the buckram brim and hand stitch in place.

5 With r.s.f., seam the two short ends of the velvet crown to form a tube. Repeat with the lining. Press.

Bi

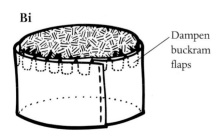

Dampen buckram flaps

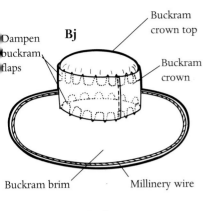

Bj

Dampen buckram flaps

Buckram crown top

Buckram crown

Buckram brim

Millinery wire

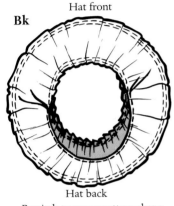

Hat front

Bk

Hat back

Restitch to paper pattern shape and trim away shaded area

6 R.s.f., sew the circular velvet crown top to the top of the crown tube. Repeat with the lining. Clip seams and press.

7 R.s.f., ease the velvet brim onto the bottom of the crown tube and stitch in place. Clip seam.

8 Put the buckram hat shape inside the velvet hat, pull the velvet well down and carefully stitch to the buckram round the edge of the brim taking care not to catch the millinery wire. (A zip foot is useful here.)

9 R.s.f., seam the brim lining pieces together to form a large continuous loop. Press.

10 Gather along both long edges and pull up to fit hat brim.

11 (Bk) Place brim pattern on to ruching and mark round the inside circle using tailor's chalk. Stitch on this line using a short stitch length. (Again the zip foot is used.) Cut away the excess fabric.

12 With r.s.f., stitch the ruched brim to the lining.

13 Put the lining inside the hat and tack the ruching in place around the edge of the brim.

14 To bind the edge of the brim cut a 3cm (1¼in) wide length of taffeta on the bias and, with r.s.f., stitch it around the top of the brim through all layers. Turn to the w.s., fold under a narrow hem and hand stitch in place.

15 Decorate the hat with feathers and flowers. Optional: cut a length of taffeta 10cm (4in) x 115cm (45in) and fold in half lengthways. With r.s.f., sew around the edge leaving an opening for turning. Turn to the r.s. and make five or six large loops. Gather the bottom of the loops together and sew to the hat brim. Intersperse with feathers and flowers.

16 Fix the hat to the doll's head with a fancy hatpin.

Dress★★

Ribbon weaving was a popular Victorian craft, and this dress has a lace-trimmed bib of woven ribbon on the bodice front. The back-fastening bodice is self lined and has a dropped waistline. The narrow sleeves are decorated with chevrons of braid, ribbon and lace. The skirt has a deep-pleated frill at the hem and the shorter overskirt has a V-shaped front panel, again decorated with chevrons of lace, ribbon and braid echoing the shape of the ribbon weaving.

Materials and notions

1.05m (41in) silk dupion 115cm (45in) wide
2.20m (87in) cotton lace 3cm (1¼in) wide
2.30m (91in) braid
3.5m (138in) lace 1cm (³⁄₈in) wide
1.60m (63in) petersham ribbon 0.5cm (¼in) wide
2m (79in) double-edged cotton lace 1.5cm (⁵⁄₈in) wide (to neaten the top of the pleats on the skirt)
Sewing thread to match
Five hooks and eyes
Small beads and pearl drops

Materials for the ribbon weaving

18cm (7in) iron-on interfacing 15cm (6in) wide
Approximately 10m (390in) ribbon, in a variety of shades in 2mm (⅛in) and 5mm (¼in) widths

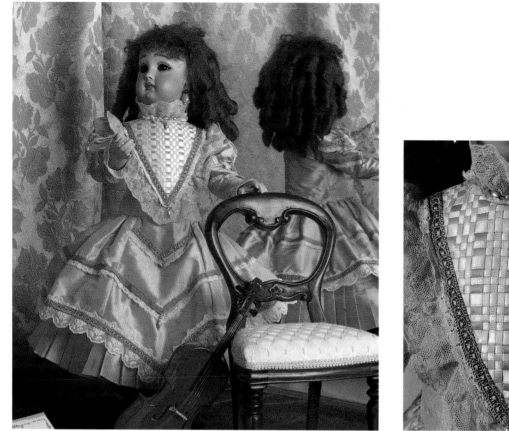

Bl

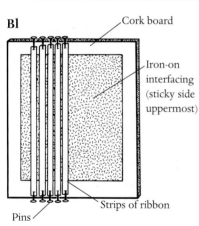

Cork board

Iron-on interfacing (sticky side uppermost)

Strips of ribbon

Pins

Bm

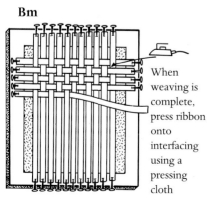

When weaving is complete, press ribbon onto interfacing using a pressing cloth

Pattern pieces There are seven pattern pieces for the dress, numbered B13, B14, B16, B17 and B19 to B21, one for the bib, numbered B15, and a pleating guide numbered B18.

Making instructions

Woven ribbon bib

1 Place the piece of iron-on interfacing, sticky side up, on to a board which can be pinned into easily – a cork mat or a thick cake board, but not polystyrene.

2 (Bl) Start by pinning the first upright ribbon 1cm (⅜in) from the side edge of the interfacing, continue across the interfacing leaving small spaces, about a pin's width, between each ribbon. Each ribbon should be cut so that it just clears the edge of the interfacing at the top and bottom. Leave 1cm (⅜in) of interfacing showing after the last upright ribbon.

3 (Bm) When all the upright ribbons are in place and the interfacing is covered except at the side edges, start weaving the horizontal ribbons. The first row is woven 1cm (⅜in) from the top. Weave *under one ribbon, over one ribbon* repeat from * to * to the end.

4 (Bm) The second row is woven *over one ribbon, under one ribbon* repeat from * to * to the end.

5 Continue repeating these two rows until the last woven row is 1cm (⅜in) from the bottom.

6 Check that all your ribbons are lying straight. Press, using a pressing cloth so that the ribbons adhere to the interfacing. (A small travelling iron fits between the pins.)

7 Remove all pins and press the edges. Turn the weaving over and press the back. The woven ribbon can now be treated as a piece of fabric.

8 Cut to shape using the ribbon bib guide.

Dress

1 (Bn) Gather a 50cm (20in) length of wide lace and, with r.s.f., sew to the side edges of the ribbon overlay (top gathered edge of lace to raw edge of ribbons).

2 R.s f., and enclosing the lace, sew the bib lining to the ribbon bib leaving the neck and shoulder edges open for turning. Clip, turn and press.

3 Sew a length of narrow flat lace on the edge of the ribbon weaving and sew a length of braid just inside this.

4 (Bo) Tack the ribbon bib to the bodice front along the shoulders and around the neck (the wide lace will be left free).

5 (Bo) R.s.f., sew bodice front to bodice back at shoulders, taking care not to catch the wide lace in the seam. Press.

6 Repeat with the bodice lining.

7 (Bp) Sew the chevron decoration on the sleeves as indicated on the pattern. The top row is narrow lace with braid above it, the middle row is narrow lace with ribbon above it and the bottom row is the same as the top row.

8 Gather the sleeve headings between notches, and pull up to fit armholes.

9 With r.s.f., sew the sleeves into the armholes

10 Matching chevrons and armhole seams, and with r.s.f., sew up the sleeve seam and down the bodice side seam. Repeat with the other side.

11 Repeat Instructions 8-10 with the lining.

12 Tack a row of gathered narrow lace around the neck on the r.s. and then a row of gathered wide lace on top of the narrow lace. The wide lace will stand up when the dress is finished.

13 R.s.f., and enclosing the rows of lace, sew the bodice to the bodice lining, up one back edge around the neck and down the other back edge. Clip seams, turn to the r.s. and press.

14 Push sleeve linings into sleeves, turn in a small hem at the wrist edge of the sleeves and sleeve linings, and insert a length of wide gathered lace between them; hand stitch them together.

15 R.s.f., seam the two skirt frill pieces together to form a circle. Press seams open.

16 Press the frill in half lengthways then press into small pleats following the skirt pleating guide (B18). Hold the pleats in place with a row of stitching sewn just inside the raw edges.

17 Trim the skirt to fit the pleats plus a seam allowance.

18 Sew a French seam down the centre back of the skirt remembering to leave a small opening at the waist edge.

19 (Bq) R.s.f., and raw edges level, stitch the pleated frill around the bottom of the skirt. Neaten this seam by sewing a row of narrow lace over the raw edges on the w.s. Optional: sew a row of lace to the r.s. where the frill meets the skirt.

20 (Br) Stitch the top chevron decoration on the overskirt front panel as indicated on the pattern – a row of narrow lace with a row of braid above it.

21 R.s.f., and matching notches, stitch the front panel to the overskirt using a French seam. Press.

22 R.s.f, sew up the back seam of the overskirt, again with a French seam, leaving a small opening at the waist edge. Press.

23 Turn under a narrow hem to the w.s. of the bottom edge and stitch in place.

24 Sew a row of flat wide lace to the r.s. of the hem.

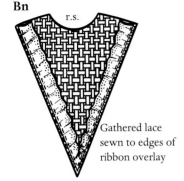

Bn

r.s.

Gathered lace sewn to edges of ribbon overlay

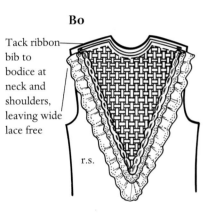

Bo

Tack ribbon bib to bodice at neck and shoulders, leaving wide lace free

r.s.

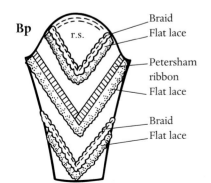

Bp

r.s.

Braid
Flat lace

Petersham ribbon

Flat lace

Braid
Flat lace

Bq

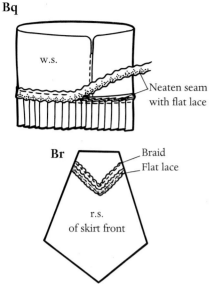

w.s.

Neaten seam
with flat lace

Br

Braid
Flat lace

r.s.
of skirt front

25 Sew a row of braid along the lace.

26 Sew the middle row of decoration round the skirt (a row of narrow lace with a row of ribbon above) following the placement line on the front panel and continue the line round the back of the skirt. You may find it helpful to press a crease 5.5cm (2¼in) from the hem to follow when sewing on the middle row of decoration.

27 Gather the skirt to fit the bodice.

28 Gather the overskirt to fit the bodice.

29 Put the skirt inside the overskirt and tack together around the waist. With r.s.f., and raw edges together, stitch the skirts to the bodice, leaving a small overlap on the bodice for fastening and taking care not to catch the bodice lining.

30 Turn under a narrow hem to the w.s. of the bodice lining and hand stitch in place.

31 Stitch five hooks and eyes, evenly spaced, to fasten the bodice back.

Waist petticoat★

Bs

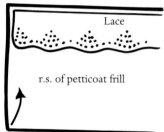

Lace

r.s. of petticoat frill

Fold upwards

Bt

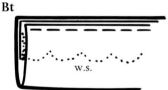

w.s.

Bu

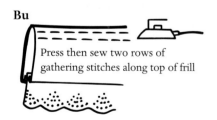

Press then sew two rows of
gathering stitches along top of frill

Bv

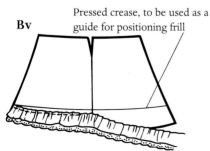

Pressed crease, to be used as a
guide for positioning frill

The petticoat is self lined and back fastening. It has a lace-covered flat front panel with a cascade of lace-edged waterfall frills at the back and sides.

Materials and notions
65cm (26in) very fine silk 115cm (45in) wide
20cm (8in) lace fabric 20cm (8in) wide (for the front overlay)
1.20m (47in) ribbon 5mm (¼in) wide
Sewing thread to match
50cm (20in) tape
Small beads
3m (118in) cotton lace 3cm (1¼in) wide

Pattern pieces There are five pattern pieces for the waist petticoat, numbered B22 to B26.

Making instructions

1 (Bs; Bt) Place the top straight edge of a length of lace along the raw edge on the r.s. of a skirt frill. Fold the frill in half lengthways enclosing the lace and seam through all layers.

2 (Bu) Turn to the r.s. and press. Repeat with the other two skirt frills.

3 (Bu) Sew two rows of gathering threads along each frill top.

4 R.s.f., seam up the petticoat back seam leaving a 5cm (2in) opening at the waist edge. Repeat with the lining and press.

5 Press a fold guide line on the skirt back 3cm (1¼in) from the bottom. This makes sewing the frills on easier.

6 (Bv) Pull up a frill to fit the skirt back and place the top of the gathered frill on the fold line on the r.s. of the skirt back and stitch in place.

7 Press a second guide line 4cm (1½in) from the top of the sewn frill.

8 Pull up another frill to fit the skirt back and sew in place with the frill top touching the fold line.

9 Press a third guide line 4cm (1½in) from the top of the second frill.

10 Pull up the last skirt frill to fit the back and sew in place with the frill top touching the fold line.

11 (Bw) Sew a length of flat lace to cover the top of this frill.

12 (Bw) Sew a length of ribbon along the bottom of the lace.

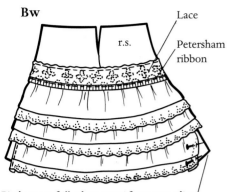

Bw

Lace

r.s.

Petersham ribbon

Pin bottom frill edges away from seam line

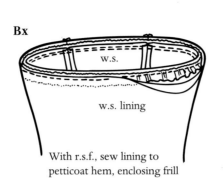

Bx

w.s.

w.s. lining

With r.s.f., sew lining to petticoat hem, enclosing frill

By

Leaving front panel flat, pull up waist to fit waistband

13 (Bw) Turn in and stitch a very narrow hem along the short edges of the bottom skirt frill. Pin these edges away from the seam line.

14 Tack the lace overlay to the r.s. of the front panel.

15 With r.s.f., sew the front panel to the skirt back taking care not to catch the sides of the bottom skirt frill.

16 Make the hem frill in the same manner as the skirt frills but omit the lace. Gather and pull up to fit the bottom of the skirt. With the gathered edge of the frill level with the hem of the skirt and, r.s.f., sew the frill to the hem making an overlapping seam at the centre back.

17 R.s.f., sew the lining front panel to the lining back. Press.

18 (Bx) R.s.f., sew the petticoat to the lining around the hem, (raw edges level and enclosing the hem frill). Turn to the r.s.

19 Hand sew a length of ribbon down either side of the front panel. Sew a bow at the bottom edge of each length of ribbon.

20 (By) Leaving the front panel flat gather the waist edge of the petticoat back and pull up to fit the waistband.

21 R.s.f., sew the waistband to the skirt waist through all layers. Turn the waistband over to the w.s., turn under a narrow hem and hand stitch in place leaving ends open.

22 To fasten, thread tape through the waistband.

23 Optional: decorate the front panel with tiny beads.

Camisole★

The back-fastening lined camisole has lace shoulder straps and a lace front trim which is decorated with tiny beads. The front is overlaid with lace fabric.

Materials and notions
15cm (6in) fine silk 115cm (45in) wide
15cm (6in) lace fabric 18cm (7in) wide – for the overlay
50cm (20in) cotton lace 3cm (1¼in) wide
50cm (20in) narrow ribbon 5mm (¼in) wide
Tiny beads
Sewing thread to match
Two hooks and eyes
Beads

Pattern pieces There are two pattern pieces for the camisole, numbered B27 and B28.

Bz

r.s.

Tack lace overlay to front

Baa

w.s.

Stitch around edge, leaving bottom open for turning

130

Bbb

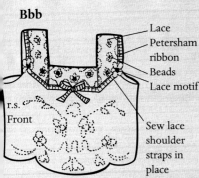

Lace
Petersham
ribbon
Beads
Lace motif

r.s.
Front

Sew lace
shoulder
straps in
place

Bcc

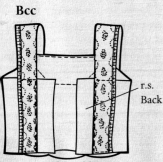

r.s.
Back

Back view of shoulder straps

Making instructions

1. Press up and stitch a small single hem at the bottom of the camisole front.
2. (Bz) Tack the lace overlay to the front. The bottom edge of the lace in the photograph has a self-finished edge. If yours has a raw edge, press it under with the hem.
3. R.s.f., stitch the side seams. Repeat with the lining and press.
4. (Baa) With r.s.f., raw edges level and matching side seams, sew the camisole to the lining from the side seam towards the back all around the edge finishing at the other side seam, leaving the bottom front edge open for turning. Clip seams, turn to the r.s. and press.
5. (Bbb; Bcc) Sew lace shoulder straps as indicated in the pattern.
6. (Bbb; Bcc) Two lace flowers have been cut from the lace overlay fabric and hand stitched to the front of the straps.
7. (Bbb; Bcc) Turn under a narrow hem to the w.s. on the bottom of the front lining and hand stitch to the front hem.
8. (Bbb; Bcc) Sew a row of ribbon around the bottom of the lace at the neckline, over the shoulders and down the back.
9. Decorate the front with small beads and stitch a bow in the centre of the neckline.
10. Sew two hooks and eyes to fasten the back.

Drawers★

The loose-fitting drawers are self lined and lace edged. They fasten at the back with tape and the bottoms of the legs are drawn up with ribbon ties.

Materials and notions

25cm (10in) very fine silk 115cm (45in) wide
1.20m (47in) cotton lace 3cm (1¼in) wide
80cm (32in) ribbon 5cm (2¼in) wide
50cm (20in) narrow tape
Sewing thread to match

Pattern pieces There is one pattern piece for the drawers, numbered B29.

Bdd

Waist casing

Leg casing

Making instructions

1. Make a buttonhole on each leg front as marked. Do not make buttonholes in the lining. If your fabric is very fine, it may be easier to stitch these by hand.
2. R.s.f., sew up the leg seams on the drawers and press. Repeat with the lining.
3. R.s.f., sew the lace around the bottom of the legs. The top straight edge of the lace is against the raw edge at the bottom of the leg.
4. R.s.f., sew up the crotch seam on the drawers, leaving a small opening at the waist edge of the back as indicated on the pattern. Press. Repeat with the lining.
5. With r.s.f., put the lining inside the drawers and with raw edges level seam around the waist. Turn to the r.s. and press.
6. With the lining inside the drawers make the casing for the ribbon by sewing a row of stitching around the waist 1cm (⅜in) down from the top.
7. (Bdd) Turn in a narrow hem on the main fabric and on the lining, at the bottom of each leg. Enclosing the raw edges hand stitch in place.
8. Make a casing by sewing two rows of stitching around each leg as indicated on the pattern. An optional row of lace can be sewn to each leg when sewing the bottom row of casing stitching.
9. Thread ribbon through the leg casings and tape through the waist.

Socks⋆

The socks are hand-knitted in cotton. The legs of the socks have a lacy pattern and the feet are in st.st.

Materials

One ball No. 8 cotton perlé
One pair 1.5mm knitting needles
Sewing-up needle

Making instructions

For abbreviations see page 9.
Cast on 49 sts, and knit 8 rows in k1, p1 rib
Work the pattern as follows:
Row 1: (K1, yf, sl 1, k2tog, psso, yf), rep to last st, k1
Row 2: P
Rep these 2 rows until the sock reaches from the knee to the ankle.

Foot shaping

K33, turn
P17, turn
Continue in st.st. on these 17 sts for a further 22 rows ending with a p row
Next row: K the 17 sts, pick up and k 12 sts from the side of the foot and continue to k the 16 sts from the left needle (45 sts)
Next row: P45, pick up and p 12 sts from along the side of the foot and continue to p along the 16 sts on the left needle (73 sts)

Heel shaping

Knit 4 rows in st.st.
5th row: K2tog, k32, k2tog, k1, k2tog, k32
6th row: P2tog, p30, p2tog, p1, p2tog, p30, p2tog
7th row: K2tog, k28, k2tog, k1, k2tog, k28, k2tog
8th row: P2tog, p26, p2tog, p1, p2tog, p26, p2tog
9th row: K2tog, k24, k2tog, k1, k2tog, k24, k2tog

10th row: P2tog, p22, p2tog, p1, p2tog, p22, p2tog
11th row: K2tog, k20, k2tog, k1, k2tog, k20, k2tog
Cast off

Hand sew the foot and back leg seam.
Repeat the instructions for the second sock.

Boots★★

The soft leather boots are knee length and fasten at the side with tiny buttons.

Materials and notions
24cm (9½in) soft leather 16cm (6½in) wide for the boot uppers
20cm (8in) soft leather 8cm (3in) wide for the contrasting fringes
10cm (4in) stiff leather 8cm (3in) wide for the soles and heels
Two motifs
Eight small buttons or beads to fasten boots
Stiff card for the insoles
Thin card for the sole infills
Contact adhesive
Sewing thread to match

Pattern pieces
There are seven pattern pieces for the boots, numbered B30 to B36.

Making instructions
Note: If the leather sticks and does not travel freely under the foot of your sewing machine, place a strip of paper under the leather. Remove it when you have completed the sewing.

1 Top stitch the buttonhole flap as marked on the pattern.
2 Place the w.s. of the buttonhole side flap on the r.s. of the outside boot leg matching notches and following the placement line on the pattern – a small spot of glue on the notch makes this easier.
3 With r.s.f., seam the inside boot leg to the outside boot leg from knee to toe.
4 R.s.f., seam the back of the boot from knee to heel.
5 Press open the seams with your fingers and glue flat to the inside of the boot, turn to the r.s.
6 Put a layer of glue on the shaded area of the cardboard sole and put the sole, sticky side out, into the bottom of the boot 6mm (¼in) from the cut edge of the leather.
7 Carefully bend the 6mm (¼in) of leather over the cardboard sole and press on to the glue, easing the fullness around the toe area.
8 Stick the thin card infill to the cardboard sole between the edges of the leather.
9 Stick the leather sole in place.
10 Stick the heel to the leather sole.
11 Punch buttonholes as marked and sew buttons or beads to fasten.
12 Repeat with the other boot.
13 (Bee) Stick the contrast fringing round the ankles and the motifs to the toes of the boots.

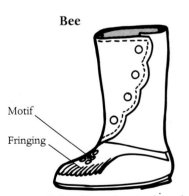

Bee

Motif

Fringing

Finished boot showing fringed decoration and front motif

Handbag★

Materials and notions
16cm (6½in) leather 13cm (5in) wide
10cm (4in) lace
Beads for decoration
One motif
Sewing thread to match

Bff

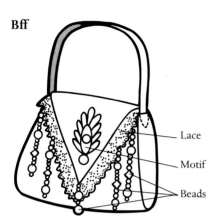

- Lace
- Motif
- Beads

Pattern pieces There are three pattern pieces for the handbag, numbered B37 to B39.

Making instructions

You may prefer to hand sew the bag but if you are machining the gussets, the machine will stitch better if you place a piece of paper under the seam. Tear the paper away when stitching is complete.

1 Sew the ends of the handle to the top of the side gussets, r.s of handle against w.s. of gusset.

2 With r.s.f., and matching notches, sew the side gussets to the bag. Turn to the r.s.

3 Sew or stick the lace around the edge of the flap.

4 Decorate the flap by sewing rows of beads at intervals along the lace.

5 (Bff) Stick or sew the motif to the centre of the flap.

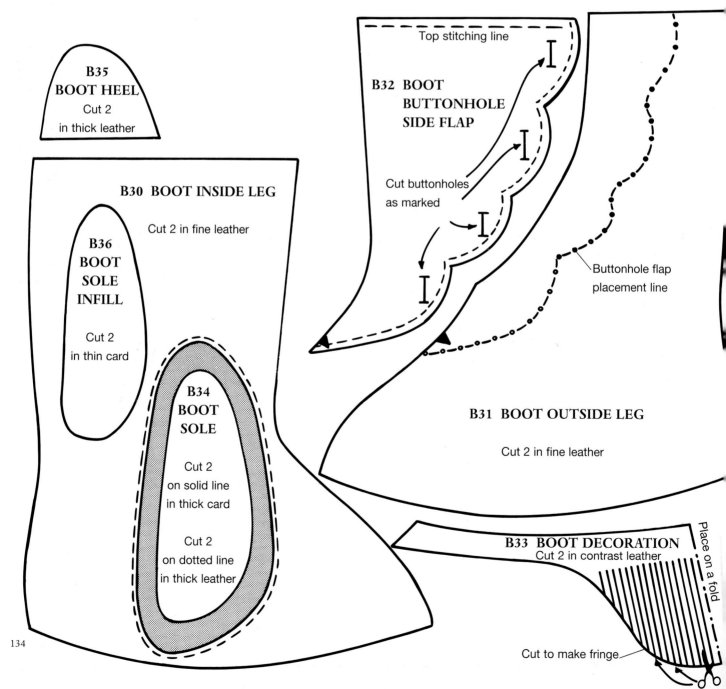

Top stitching line

B32 BOOT BUTTONHOLE SIDE FLAP

Cut buttonholes as marked

Buttonhole flap placement line

B35 BOOT HEEL
Cut 2
in thick leather

B30 BOOT INSIDE LEG

Cut 2 in fine leather

B36 BOOT SOLE INFILL

Cut 2 in thin card

B34 BOOT SOLE

Cut 2 on solid line in thick card

Cut 2 on dotted line in thick leather

B31 BOOT OUTSIDE LEG

Cut 2 in fine leather

B33 BOOT DECORATION
Cut 2 in contrast leather

Place on a fold

Cut to make fringe

134

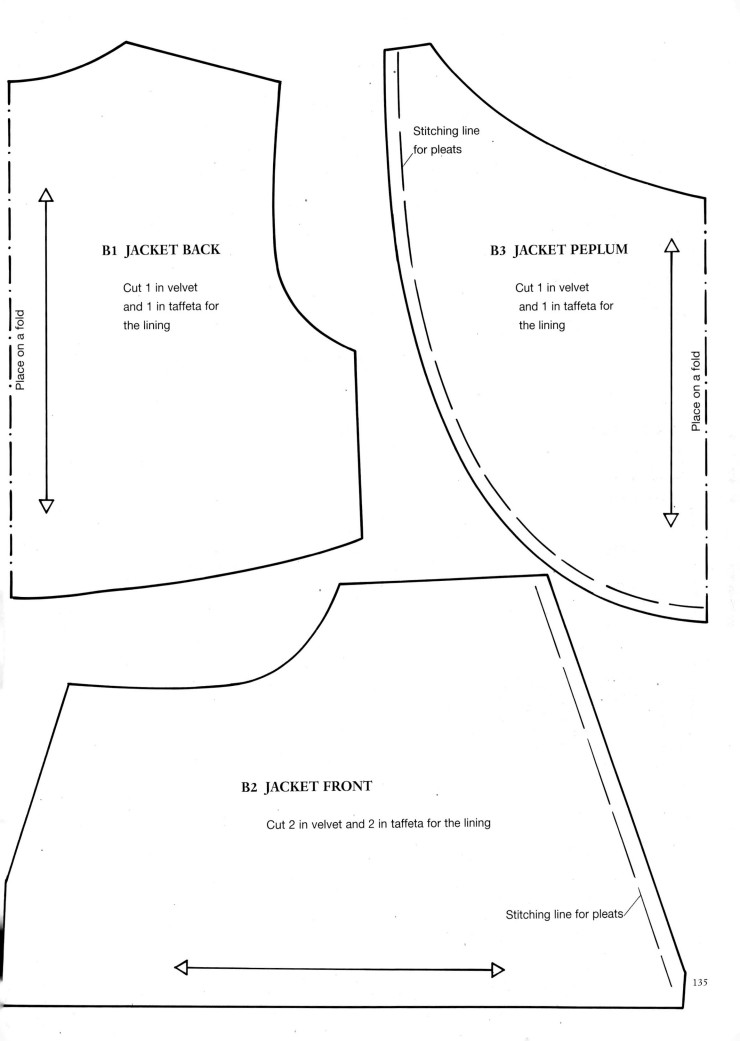

B1 JACKET BACK

Cut 1 in velvet
and 1 in taffeta for
the lining

Place on a fold

Stitching line
for pleats

B3 JACKET PEPLUM

Cut 1 in velvet
and 1 in taffeta for
the lining

Place on a fold

B2 JACKET FRONT

Cut 2 in velvet and 2 in taffeta for the lining

Stitching line for pleats

135

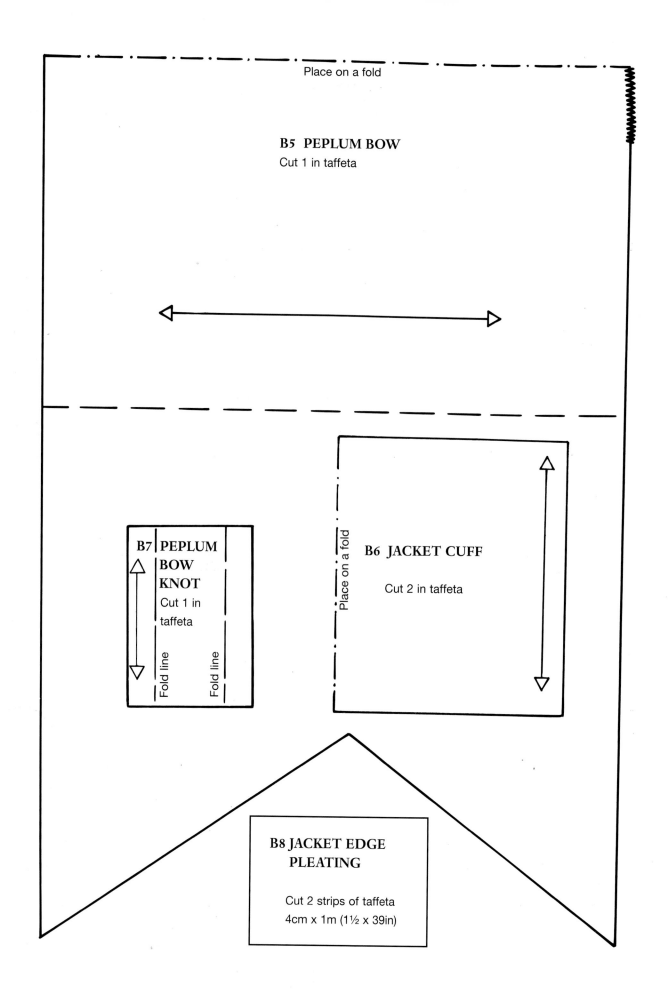

Place on a fold

B5 PEPLUM BOW

Cut 1 in taffeta

B7 PEPLUM BOW KNOT

Cut 1 in taffeta

Fold line   Fold line

Place on a fold

B6 JACKET CUFF

Cut 2 in taffeta

B8 JACKET EDGE PLEATING

Cut 2 strips of taffeta
4cm x 1m (1½ x 39in)

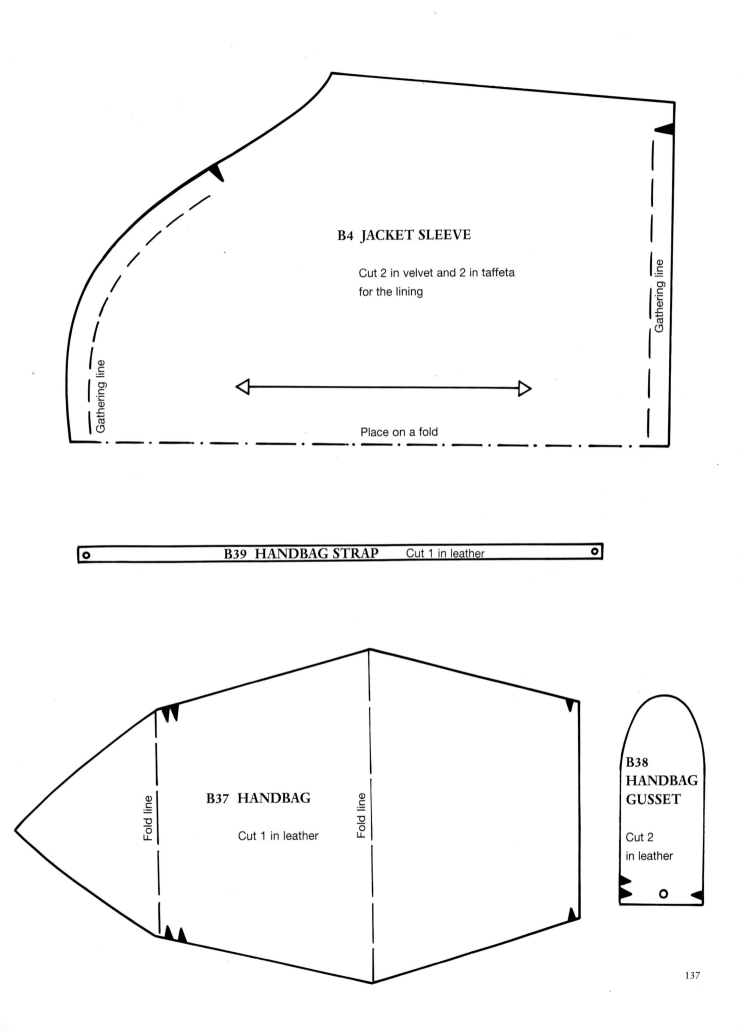

B4 JACKET SLEEVE

Cut 2 in velvet and 2 in taffeta
for the lining

Gathering line

Gathering line

Place on a fold

B39 HANDBAG STRAP   Cut 1 in leather

Fold line

Fold line

B37 HANDBAG

Cut 1 in leather

**B38
HANDBAG
GUSSET**

Cut 2
in leather

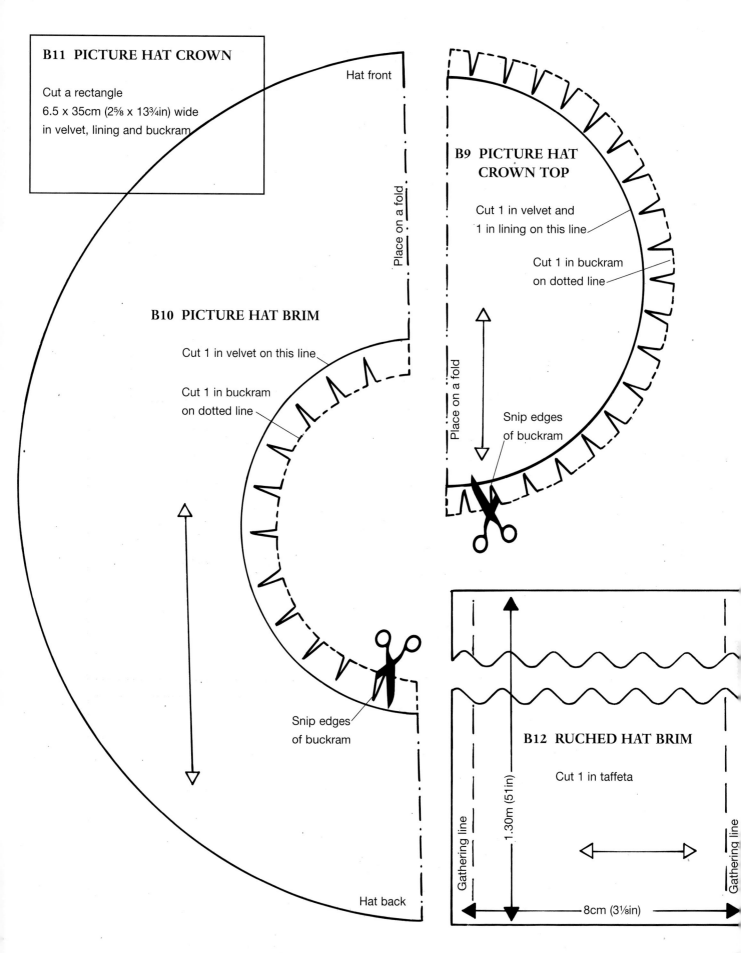

B11 PICTURE HAT CROWN

Cut a rectangle
6.5 x 35cm (2⅝ x 13¾in) wide
in velvet, lining and buckram

Hat front

Place on a fold

B9 PICTURE HAT CROWN TOP

Cut 1 in velvet and
1 in lining on this line

Cut 1 in buckram
on dotted line

Place on a fold

Snip edges
of buckram

B10 PICTURE HAT BRIM

Cut 1 in velvet on this line

Cut 1 in buckram
on dotted line

Snip edges
of buckram

Hat back

B12 RUCHED HAT BRIM

Cut 1 in taffeta

Gathering line

1.30m (51in)

Gathering line

8cm (3⅛in)

138

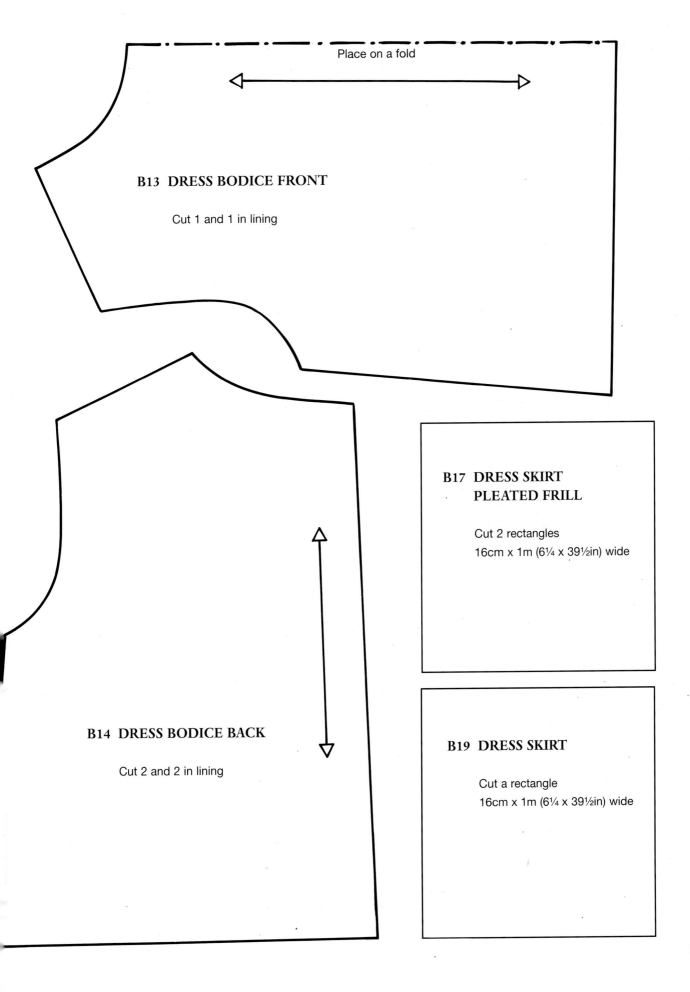

Place on a fold

B13 DRESS BODICE FRONT

Cut 1 and 1 in lining

**B17 DRESS SKIRT
PLEATED FRILL**

Cut 2 rectangles
16cm x 1m (6¼ x 39½in) wide

B14 DRESS BODICE BACK

Cut 2 and 2 in lining

B19 DRESS SKIRT

Cut a rectangle
16cm x 1m (6¼ x 39½in) wide

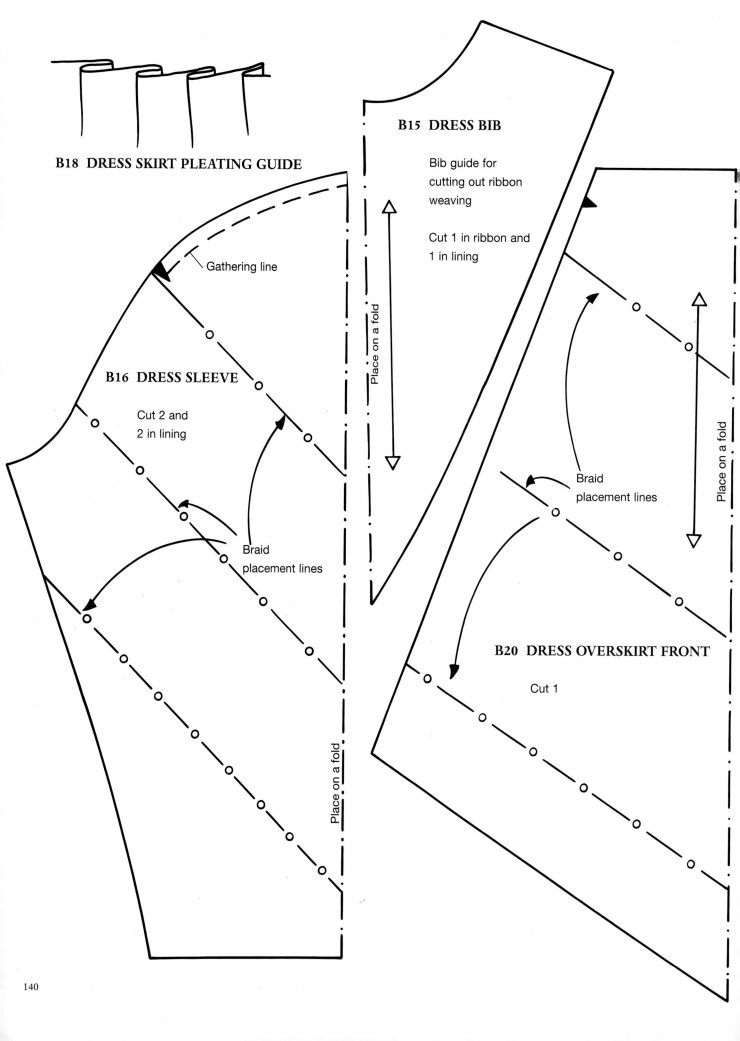

B18 DRESS SKIRT PLEATING GUIDE

B15 DRESS BIB

Bib guide for
cutting out ribbon
weaving

Cut 1 in ribbon and
1 in lining

Place on a fold

Gathering line

B16 DRESS SLEEVE

Cut 2 and
2 in lining

Braid
placement lines

Braid
placement lines

B20 DRESS OVERSKIRT FRONT

Cut 1

Place on a fold

Place on a fold

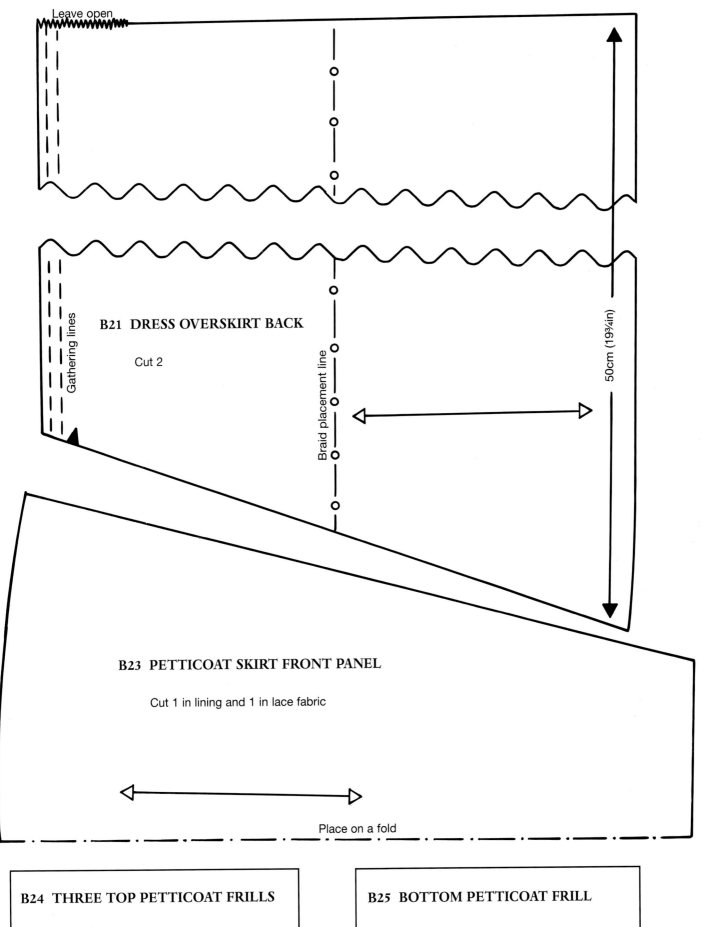

Leave open

B21 DRESS OVERSKIRT BACK

Cut 2

Gathering lines

Braid placement line

50cm (19¾in)

B23 PETTICOAT SKIRT FRONT PANEL

Cut 1 in lining and 1 in lace fabric

Place on a fold

B24 THREE TOP PETTICOAT FRILLS

Cut 3 rectangles 15 x 75cm (6 x 29½ in) wide
(use 1 per frill)

B25 BOTTOM PETTICOAT FRILL

Cut 1 rectangle 15cm x 1m (6 x 39½in) wide

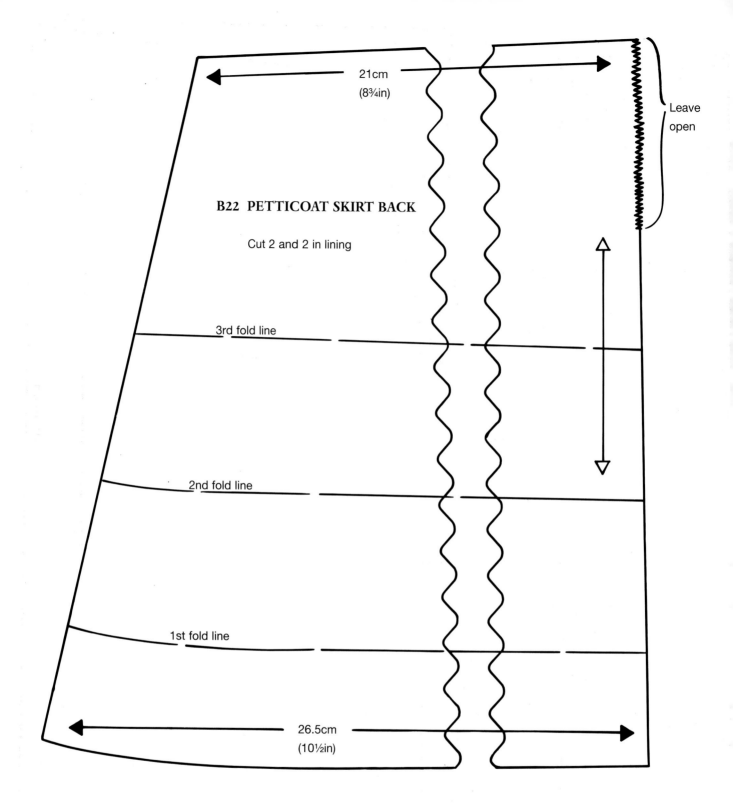

B22 PETTICOAT SKIRT BACK

Cut 2 and 2 in lining

21cm
(8¾in)

Leave
open

3rd fold line

2nd fold line

1st fold line

26.5cm
(10½in)

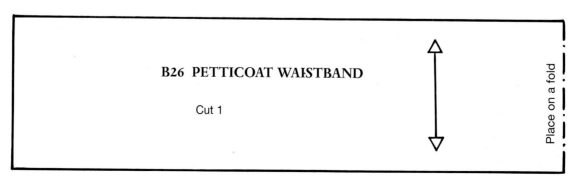

B26 PETTICOAT WAISTBAND

Cut 1

Place on a fold

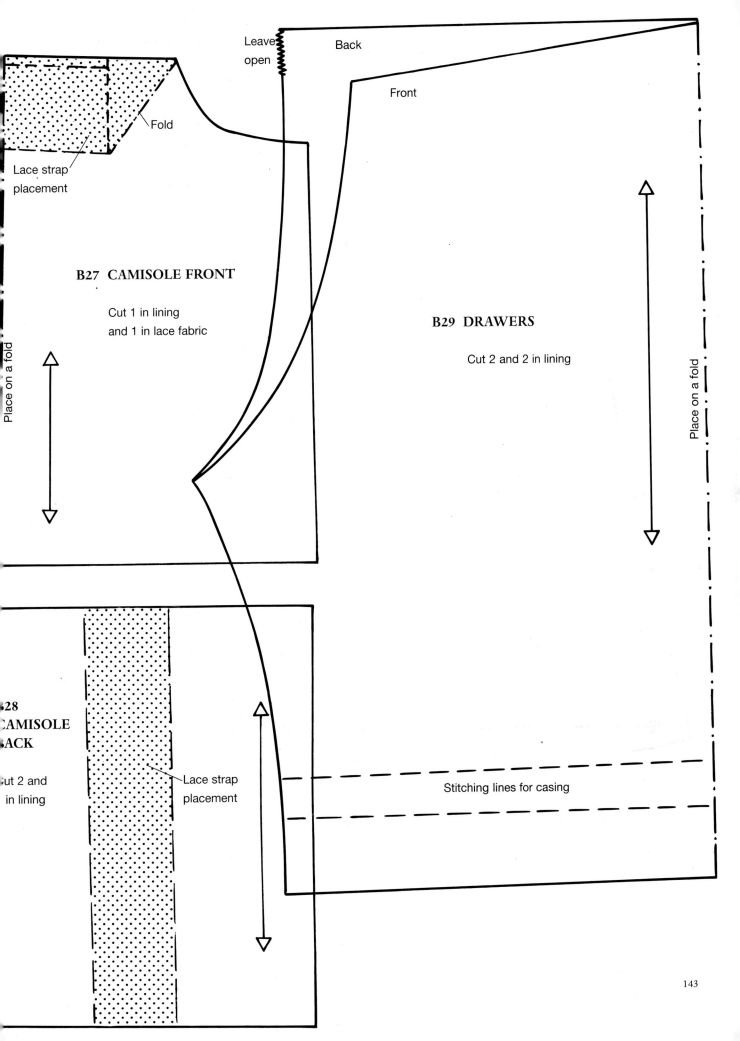

Leave open

Back

Front

Fold

Lace strap placement

B27 CAMISOLE FRONT

Cut 1 in lining
and 1 in lace fabric

Place on a fold

B29 DRAWERS

Cut 2 and 2 in lining

Place on a fold

B28
CAMISOLE
BACK

Cut 2 and
in lining

Lace strap
placement

Stitching lines for casing

143

NOELLE

Christmas party outfit

Noelle is a reproduction of the antique doll 'AT11', originally produced by the A. Thullier factory of Paris. She has a porcelain head with glass paperweight eyes, a composition body and a mohair wig. Beneath her sumptuous dress she wears a coloured satin petticoat and beneath this a red flannel petticoat. Flannel was worn in winter for its warmth. When coloured underwear was first available, it was considered rather risqué but soon became a popular fashion fad. During the nineteenth century several layers of petticoats were worn, often as many as nine or ten! Noelle's outfit consists of a party dress, satin petticoat, red flannel petticoat, camisole, pantaloons, floral circlet, socks and shoes. The dress and both petticoat bodices are lined.

Dimensions

Height: 56cm (22in)

Circumference of head: 32cm (12½in)

Waist: 27cm (10¾in)

Neck: 17cm (6¾in)

Pattern pieces

There are 20 pattern pieces for Noelle's entire outfit, numbered N1 to N20 and printed on pages 155-159.

Party dress★★

The dress bodice is back fastening and self lined. The skirt has three gathered, lace-trimmed flounces on either side. The bodice has a tucked front panel which is decorated with lace, ribbon and covered buttons. The sleeves are long and have very full puffed oversleeves. There is a wide ribbon bow on the waistline at the back of the dress.

Materials and notions

1m (39in) silk dupion 115cm (45in) wide
70cm (20in) striped fabric 115cm (45in) wide for the two top frills and oversleeves
6.5m (256in) narrow cotton lace
1m (39in) tartan ribbon 2.5cm (1in) wide
1m (39in) tartan ribbon 5cm (2in) wide for the bow
Eight small buttons to cover – the buttons in the photograph are covered with a scrap of green silk
Sewing threads to match

Pattern pieces There are ten pattern pieces for the dress, numbered N1 to N10.

Making instructions

1 Neaten all raw edges.
2 Press up a small double hem on the bottom of each frill and stitch in place. Then sew a length of narrow flat lace along the r.s. of each hem.
3 Press up a 1cm (⅜in) single hem to the w.s. at the top of the second and third frill.
4 Sew two rows of gathering stitches along the top of each frill and pull up the frills to fit along their appropriate placement lines on the skirt sides. The shortest frill is stitched at the top of the skirt side.
5 Press creases along the placement lines on the skirt sides as a guide for sewing the frills to the skirt (see pattern piece).
6 (Na) Stitch the gathered frills in place with the w.s. of frill to r.s. of skirt side.
7 With r.s.f., stitch skirt front to skirt sides catching in the edges of the frills.
8 R.s.f., sew skirt back pieces to skirt sides again sewing through the edges of the frills.
9 R.s.f., sew skirt back seam remembering to allow a small opening at the waist edge.
10 Turn the edges of the waist opening to the w.s. and hand stitch in place.
11 (Nb) Make tucks in the front bodice panel using the tuck guide (N9). Press a hem to the w.s. along the side edges of the tucked panel and stitch the panel to the r.s. of the bodice front – see placement lines on bodice front pattern.
12 (Nc) Using a long stitch length, sew a row of narrow lace down the centre of the narrow ribbon and pull up into gathers.
13 With r.s.f., sew a row of the gathered ribbon and lace down each side of the tucked panel.
14 Sew a second row of gathered ribbon and lace just inside the first row.
15 With r.s.f., sew the bodice shoulder seams. Press.
16 Repeat with the lining.
17 Fold the neckband in half lengthways, r.s.f., and seam across the short raw edges at either end. Clip, turn to the r.s. and press.

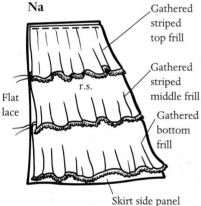

Na
Gathered striped top frill
Gathered striped middle frill
Gathered bottom frill
Flat lace
r.s.
Skirt side panel

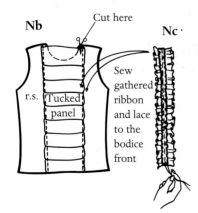

Nb
Cut here
Nc
r.s. Tucked panel
Sew gathered ribbon and lace to the bodice front

Nd

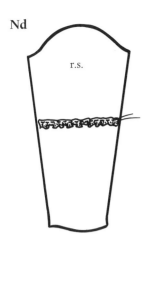

18 With r.s.f., sew the double neckband round the bodice neck, placing the centre of the neckband to the centre of the neck opening. Clip the seam.

19 (Nd) Sew a row of flat lace along the placement line on each sleeve.

20 (Ne) Gather the bottom of the oversleeve to fit across the sleeve on the placement line and, with r.s.f., tack and then stitch in place.

21 Gather the oversleeve heading to fit the sleeve heading and stitch round the sleeve heading through both layers using a long stitch. Pull up to fit the bodice armhole.

22 With r.s.f., sew sleeve to bodice around armhole.

23 (Nf) R.s.f., and matching armhole seams, sew up the side seam across the armhole seam and continue down the sleeve seam.

24 Repeat with the other sleeve.

25 Gather the heading of the sleeve lining to fit bodice lining armhole and stitch in place.

26 R.s.f., sew up bodice lining side seam across the armhole seam and down the sleeve seam. Repeat Instructions 25 and 26 with the other sleeve.

27 (Ng) With r.s.f., sew bodice to bodice lining, up the back opening, around the neck enclosing the neckband and down the other back opening. Clip seams, turn and press.

28 (Nh) Sew two rows of gathering stitches around the waist of the skirt and pull up to fit the bodice allowing a small overlap at the back for fastening.

29 R.s.f., sew the skirt to the bodice. Take care not to catch the bodice lining.

30 Turn under a small hem on the waist edge of the bodice lining and hand stitch in place.

31 Press up a double hem around the skirt and hem stitch by hand.

32 Turn the bottom edges of the sleeves and sleeve linings to the w.s. so that the raw edges are enclosed and slip stitch together by hand.

33 Make four evenly spaced buttonholes on the right hand side of the bodice back. Sew four buttons on the opposite side to correspond with the button-holes.

34 Tie the wide tartan ribbon into a bow and sew to the centre back of the waist.

35 Sew four covered buttons as decoration down the bodice front.

Ne

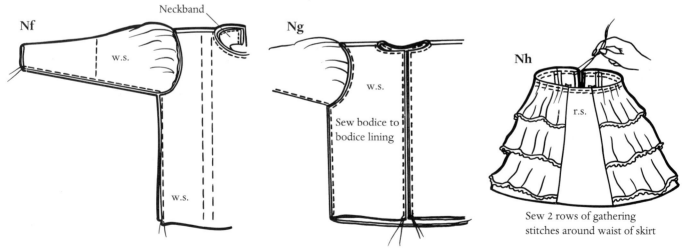

Satin petticoat★

The petticoat has a dropped waistline and gathered skirt. The skirt has a full frill at the hem which is edged with a pleated trim, and the bodice is lined with fine silk and fastens at the back. The front neckline, skirt and frill are decorated with flowered braid.

Ni

Nj

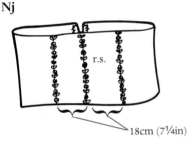

├─ 18cm (7¼in)

Nk

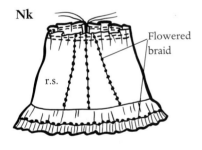

Flowered braid

r.s.

Materials and notions

70cm (28in) satin 115cm (45in) wide

55cm (22in) fine silk 115cm (45in) wide to line the bodice – this is also sufficient for the pantaloons and the camisole (page 152)

2.20m (87in) pleated trim

3m (118in) narrow flowered braid

Four hooks and eyes

Sewing thread to match

Pattern pieces There are four pattern pieces for the petticoat, numbered N1, N2 (see Dress bodice front and Dress bodice back), N11 and N12.

Making instructions

1 R.s.f., join the bodice shoulder seams, press. Repeat with the lining.

2 (Ni) With r.s.f., sew the bodice to the lining up the back, around the neck and down the other side of the back.

3 (Ni) Still with r.s.f., sew the bodice to the lining around the armholes, clip seams, turn by pulling the backs through the shoulders and press.

4 R.s.f., and armhole seams level, sew up the bodice side seam, across the armhole seam and down the bodice lining side seam. Press and turn to the r.s. Repeat with the other side.

5 (Nj) Sew the skirt pieces together to form a tube using French seams – remember to leave a small opening at the waist edge on the centre back seam. Press. Sew a row of braid down the centre front seam and a row on either side 18cm (7¼in) from the central row.

6 With r.s.f., join the frill pieces together to form a tube. Press.

7 R.s.f., sew the pleated trim around the hem of the frill. Neaten the seam. Press the seam towards the waist.

8 Stitch the flowered braid around the frill just above the pleated trim through all layers. Sew a strip of braid around the front neckline.

9 Run two rows of gathering threads around the top of the frill and pull up to fit the skirt.

10 With r.s.f., sew the frill to the skirt, neaten the raw edges and press the seam towards the waist.

11 (Nk) Gather the top of the skirt to fit the waist of the bodice allowing a small overlap for fastening. With r.s.f., stitch the skirt to the bodice, taking care not to catch the bodice lining.

12 Turn under a small hem at the waist edge of the bodice lining and, enclosing all raw edges, hand stitch in place.

13 Hand sew four hooks and eyes evenly spaced down the back opening.

Red flannel petticoat★

The flannel petticoat is similar to the satin petticoat in shape but it has a double-thickness silk frill around the bottom of the skirt.

Materials and notions

60cm (24in) red flannel 115cm (45in) wide (Brushed cotton is an acceptable substitute for fine red flannel)

14cm (5½in) silk (or red flannel) 40cm (16in) wide for the frill

20cm (8in) fine cotton 50cm (20in) wide for the bodice lining

Four hooks and eyes

Sewing thread to match

Hand embroidery thread

N1

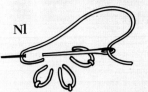

Follow these diagrams
for the hand embroidery

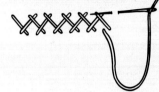

Nm

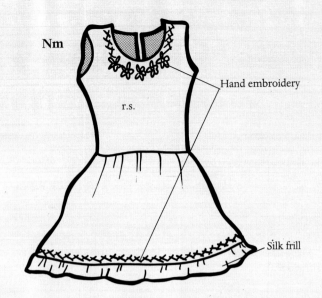

Hand embroidery

r.s.

Silk frill

Pattern pieces There are four pattern pieces for the red flannel petticoat, numbered N1, N2, N13 and N14.

Making instructions
Follow the instructions for the satin petticoat (page 149). Omit the braid in Instruction 5 and leave out Instructions 7 and 8. Remember to fold the frill in half lengthways before gathering in Instruction 9, so the frill will be a double thickness of fabric.
(N1; Nm) Hand embroider the bodice and the skirt above the frill.

Camisole★

The camisole top is made of fine silk. It has two rows of ribbon and lace down the front and fastens with small buttons.

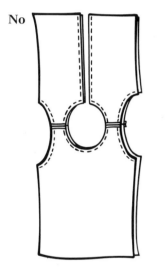

Nn

Lace ⟋ ⟍ Ribbon

Materials and notions

Fine silk – there is sufficient fabric for the camisole in the amount given for the satin petticoat lining (page 149)
30cm (12in) ribbon 1cm (⅜in) wide
30cm (12in) cotton lace
Three buttons
Sewing thread to match

Pattern pieces There are two pattern pieces for the camisole, numbered N15 and N16.

Making instructions

1 (Nn) Sew a row of lace and ribbon on the r.s. of each front as indicated on the pattern.
2 With r.s.f., sew the shoulder seams on the camisole. Press. Repeat with the lining.
3 (No) R.s.f., join the camisole to the lining up the front, around the neck then down the other front, then sew round each armhole. Clip the seams and turn to the r.s. by pulling the fronts through the shoulders. Press.
4 With r.s.f., sew up the camisole side seam across the armhole seam then down the lining side seam. Repeat with the other side and press.
5 With r.s.f., sew the camisole to the lining along the bottom edge leaving an opening for turning. Turn to the r.s., press and close the opening with hand sewing.
6 Make three buttonholes evenly spaced down the right front.
7 Sew three buttons on the left front to correspond with the buttonholes.

No

Pantaloons★

The pantaloons fasten at the back with ribbon ties. The bottoms of the legs are tucked and trimmed with lace, ribbon bows and flowered braid.

Materials and notions

Fine silk – there is sufficient fabric in the measurement given for the satin petticoat lining (page 149)
90cm (35½in) cotton lace
45cm (18in) flowered braid
70cm (27½in) ribbon 1cm (⅜in) wide
Sewing thread to match

Pattern pieces

There is one pattern piece for the pantaloons, numbered N17.

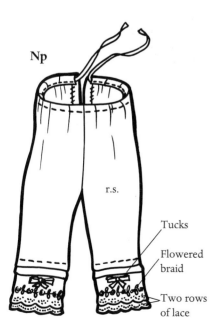

Np

r.s.

Tucks

Flowered braid

Two rows of lace

Making instructions

1 Neaten all raw edges.
2 With r.s.f., sew crotch seams leaving an opening at the waist edge on the back, press.
3 R.s.f., sew the leg seams matching crotch seams. Press.
4 Turn up a double hem at the bottom of each leg and stitch in place.
5 Turn under and stitch a double hem to the w.s. at the waist edge wide enough to take the ribbon.

6 Make tucks on the legs as indicated on the pattern. Pressing the tucks before sewing makes the sewing easier.

7 Sew two rows of lace one above the other at the bottom of each leg.

8 Sew a row of flowered braid above the lace.

9 (Np) Sew a ribbon bow in the middle of each leg.

10 Thread ribbon through the waist to fasten.

Hair decoration ★

The doll wears a half-circlet of wired flowers and ivy leaves in her hair.

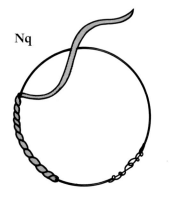

Nq

Materials and notions
Millinery wire
Wadding
1.30m (51in) 1cm (⅜in) wide satin ribbon
Silk flowers
Ivy leaves

Pattern pieces None.

Making instructions
1 Using millinery wire, make a circle to fit the doll's head.

2 (Nq) Cut a narrow strip of wadding and bind the wire circle.

3 (Nr; Ns) Using the ribbon, bind half the circle. Arrange the flowers and leaves over the rest of the circle and hold in place by continuing to bind ribbon over the stems

4 (Nt) Bend the circle to form a semi-circle.

5 Fix in place on the doll's head with hair clips.

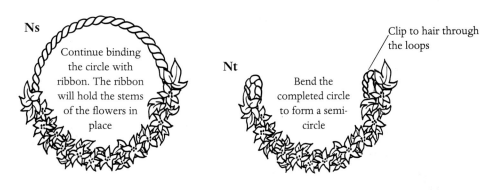

Nr

Ns

Continue binding the circle with ribbon. The ribbon will hold the stems of the flowers in place

Nt

Bend the completed circle to form a semi-circle

Clip to hair through the loops

Socks★

The cotton socks are hand-knitted in stocking stitch with a ribbed band at the top.

Materials and notions
One ball No. 5 cotton perlé
One pair 2mm knitting needles
Sewing-up needle

Making instructions
See page 9 for abbreviations.
Cast on 40 sts. and knit 6 rows in k1, p1, rib
Continue in st.st. until work measures 9cm (3½in)

Foot shaping
K27, turn
P14
Continue in st.st. on these 14 sts for a further 18 rows ending with a p row
Next row: K the 14 sts, pick up and k 13 sts from the side of the foot and continue to the 13 sts from the left needle (40 sts)
Next row: P40 sts, pick up and p 13 sts from the side of the foot and continue to p the 13 sts from the left needle (66 sts)

Heel shaping
Knit 2 rows in st.st.
3rd row: K2tog, k28, sl1, k1, psso, k2, k2tog, k28, k2tog
4th row: P2tog, p26, sl1, p1, psso, p2, p2tog, p26, p2tog
5th row: K2tog, k24, sl1, k1, psso, k2, k2tog, k24, k2tog
6th row: P2tog, p22, sl1, p1, psso, p2, p2tog, p22, p2tog
7th row: K2tog, k20, sl1, k1, psso, k2, k2tog, k20, k2tog
8th row: P2tog, p18, sl1, p1, psso, p2, p2tog, p18, p2tog
Cast off

Hand sew the foot and back leg seam.
Repeat the instructions for the second sock.

Leather shoes★

The shoes tie at the ankles with ribbon and the fronts are decorated with tassels.

Materials and notions
30cm (12in) fine leather 10cm (4in) wide for the uppers
10cm (4in) thick leather 8cm (3in) wide for the soles and heels
Thick card for the insoles, picture mounting quality
Thin card for the infills
Glue (contact adhesive)
40cm (16in) ribbon 3mm (⅛in) wide
Two tassels – cut from furnishing braid

Pattern pieces There are three pattern pieces for the shoes, numbered N18 to N20.

Making instructions
Note: If your machine will not travel freely over the leather, place paper under the piece to be sewn and tear off when stitching is complete.
 1 Top stitch around the top edge of the shoe.
 2 With r.s.f., stitch the back seam, open out and stick the seam flat.
 3 Put a layer of glue around the edge of the thick card insole as indicated by the shaded area on the pattern.
 4 (Nu) Insert the card insole into the bottom of the shoe, glue side downwards.
 5 Pull the edge of the shoe down and bend it smoothly over the glued sole. Take care when rounding off the toe.
 6 Stick the thin card infill to the insole between the edges of the leather.
 7 Glue the leather sole in place and then the heel.
 8 Punch holes in the straps and thread ribbon through them.
 9 Stick the tassel in place.
10 Repeat with the other shoe.

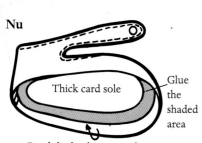

Nu

Thick card sole

Glue the shaded area

Bend the leather onto glue

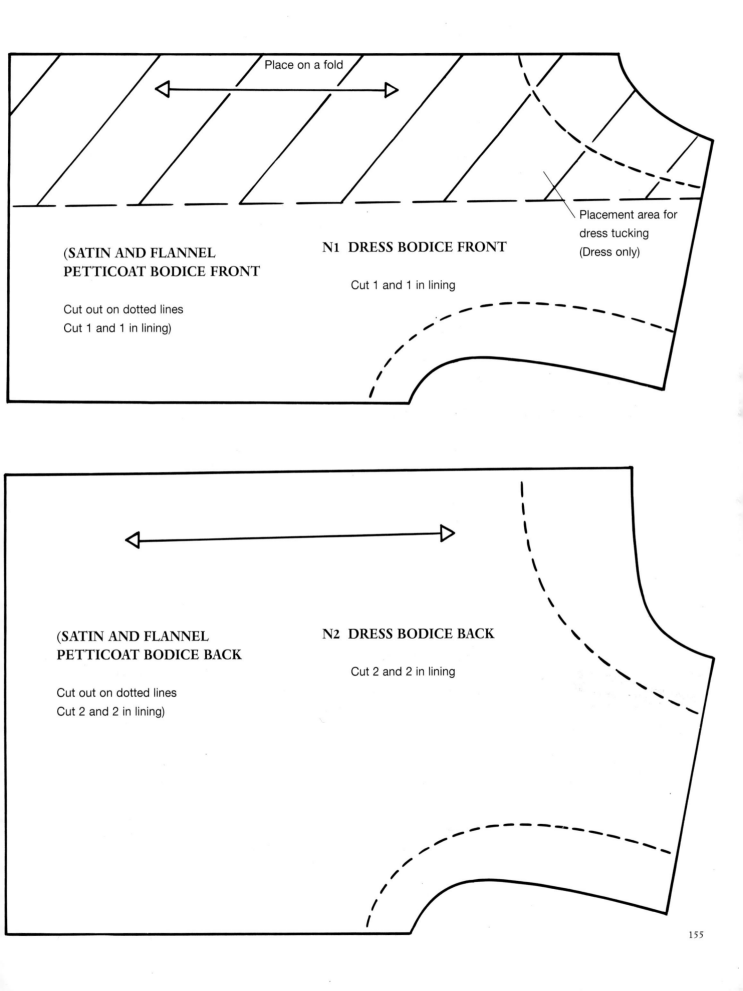

Place on a fold

(SATIN AND FLANNEL PETTICOAT BODICE FRONT

Cut out on dotted lines
Cut 1 and 1 in lining)

N1 DRESS BODICE FRONT

Cut 1 and 1 in lining

Placement area for dress tucking (Dress only)

(SATIN AND FLANNEL PETTICOAT BODICE BACK

Cut out on dotted lines
Cut 2 and 2 in lining)

N2 DRESS BODICE BACK

Cut 2 and 2 in lining

Place along a fold when cutting skirt sides

SKIRT FRONT

Cut 1 from the shaded area,
placing this edge along a fold
(ignore frill placement lines)

SKIRT BACK

Cut 2 full-size pattern pieces.
This edge is the centre back seam
(ignore frill placement lines)

This edge is back seam (no need to place along a fold))

Placement line for bottom frill on skirt sides

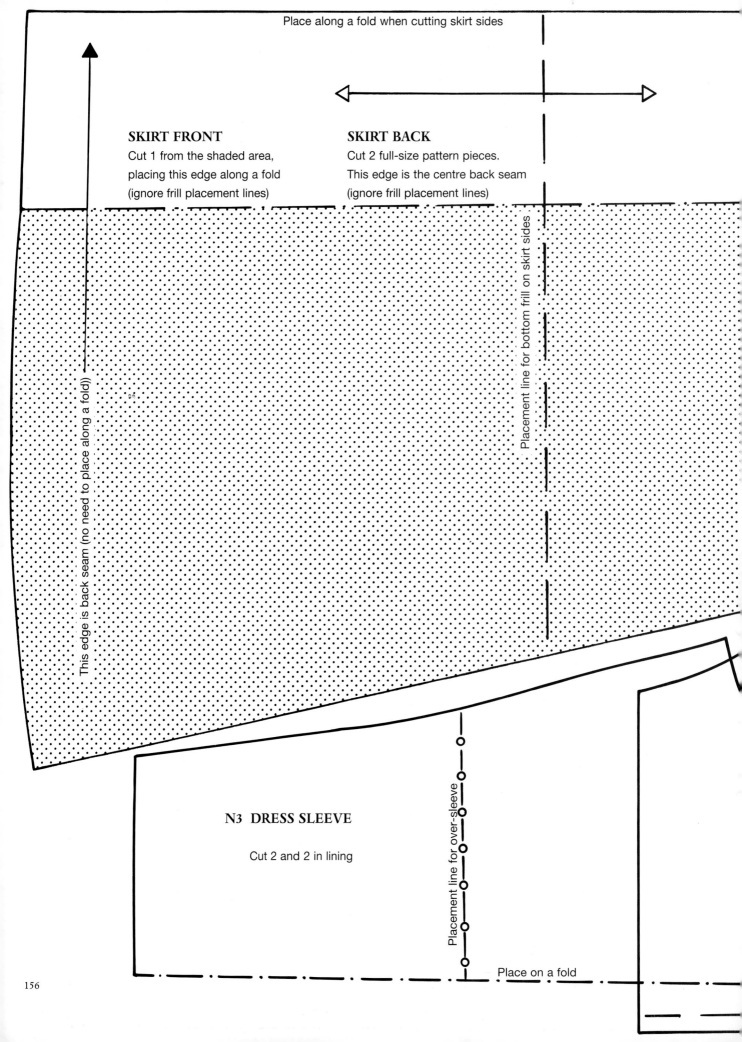

N3 DRESS SLEEVE

Cut 2 and 2 in lining

Placement line for over-sleeve

Place on a fold

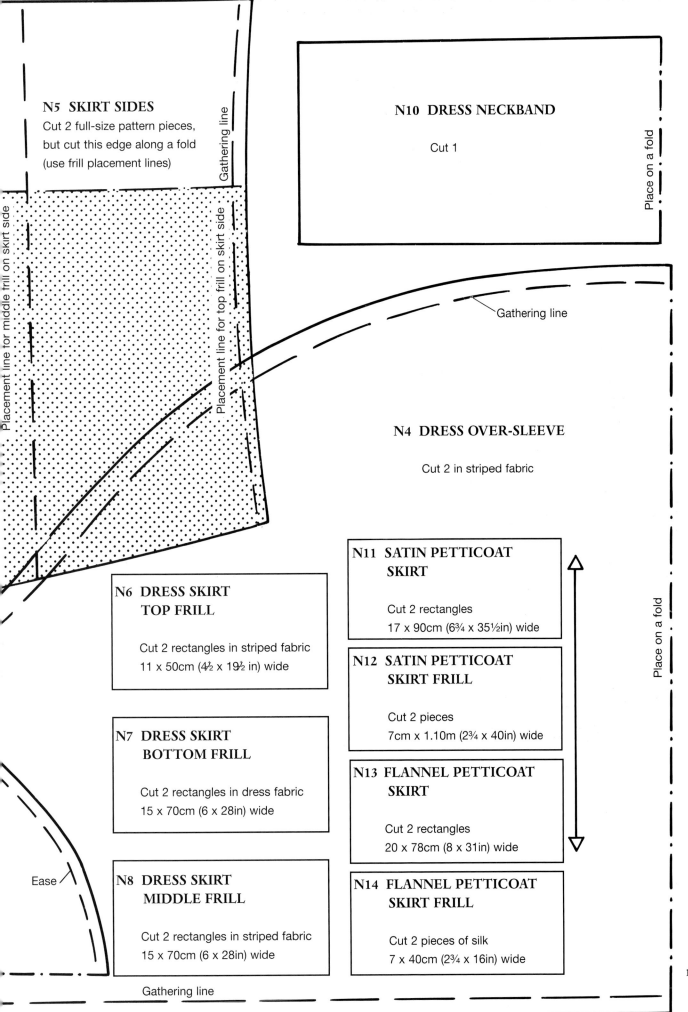

N5 SKIRT SIDES

Cut 2 full-size pattern pieces,
but cut this edge along a fold
(use frill placement lines)

Gathering line

Placement line for middle frill on skirt side

Placement line for top frill on skirt side

N10 DRESS NECKBAND

Cut 1

Place on a fold

Gathering line

N4 DRESS OVER-SLEEVE

Cut 2 in striped fabric

Place on a fold

**N11 SATIN PETTICOAT
SKIRT**

Cut 2 rectangles
17 x 90cm (6¾ x 35½in) wide

**N6 DRESS SKIRT
TOP FRILL**

Cut 2 rectangles in striped fabric
11 x 50cm (4½ x 19½ in) wide

**N12 SATIN PETTICOAT
SKIRT FRILL**

Cut 2 pieces
7cm x 1.10m (2¾ x 40in) wide

**N7 DRESS SKIRT
BOTTOM FRILL**

Cut 2 rectangles in dress fabric
15 x 70cm (6 x 28in) wide

**N13 FLANNEL PETTICOAT
SKIRT**

Cut 2 rectangles
20 x 78cm (8 x 31in) wide

Ease

**N8 DRESS SKIRT
MIDDLE FRILL**

Cut 2 rectangles in striped fabric
15 x 70cm (6 x 28in) wide

**N14 FLANNEL PETTICOAT
SKIRT FRILL**

Cut 2 pieces of silk
7 x 40cm (2¾ x 16in) wide

Gathering line

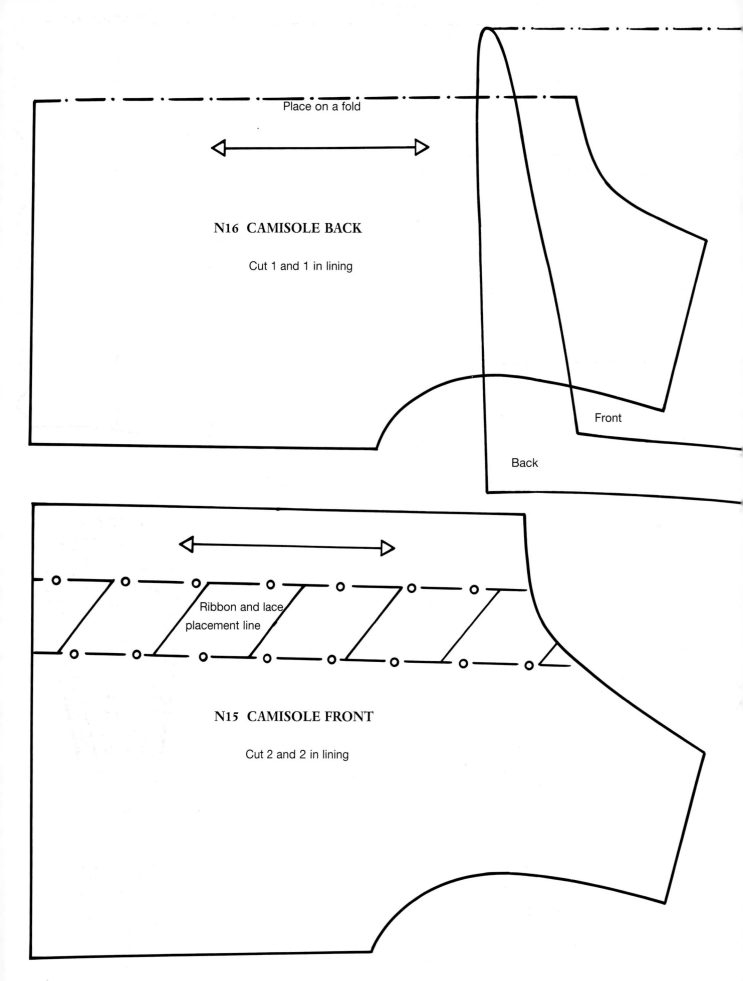

Place on a fold

N16 CAMISOLE BACK

Cut 1 and 1 in lining

Front

Back

Ribbon and lace
placement line

N15 CAMISOLE FRONT

Cut 2 and 2 in lining

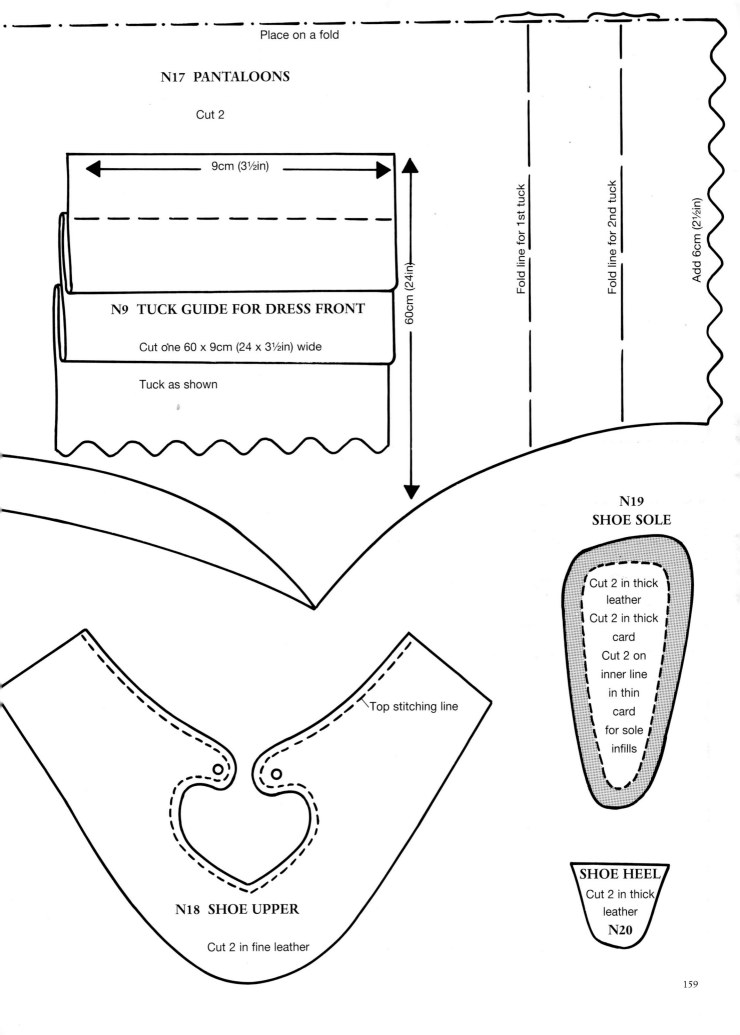

Place on a fold

N17 PANTALOONS

Cut 2

9cm (3½in)

60cm (24in)

Fold line for 1st tuck

Fold line for 2nd tuck

Add 6cm (2½in)

N9 TUCK GUIDE FOR DRESS FRONT

Cut one 60 x 9cm (24 x 3½in) wide

Tuck as shown

N19
SHOE SOLE

Cut 2 in thick leather
Cut 2 in thick card
Cut 2 on inner line in thin card for sole infills

Top stitching line

N18 SHOE UPPER

Cut 2 in fine leather

SHOE HEEL
Cut 2 in thick leather
N20

Further ideas

Once you have made some of the outfits in this book, you may want to devise patterns of your own. Pattern pieces for the boy's outfit featured on the back jacket are shown below.

Velvet Knickerbockers and Silk Shirt
to fit a 37.5cm (15in) tall boy doll

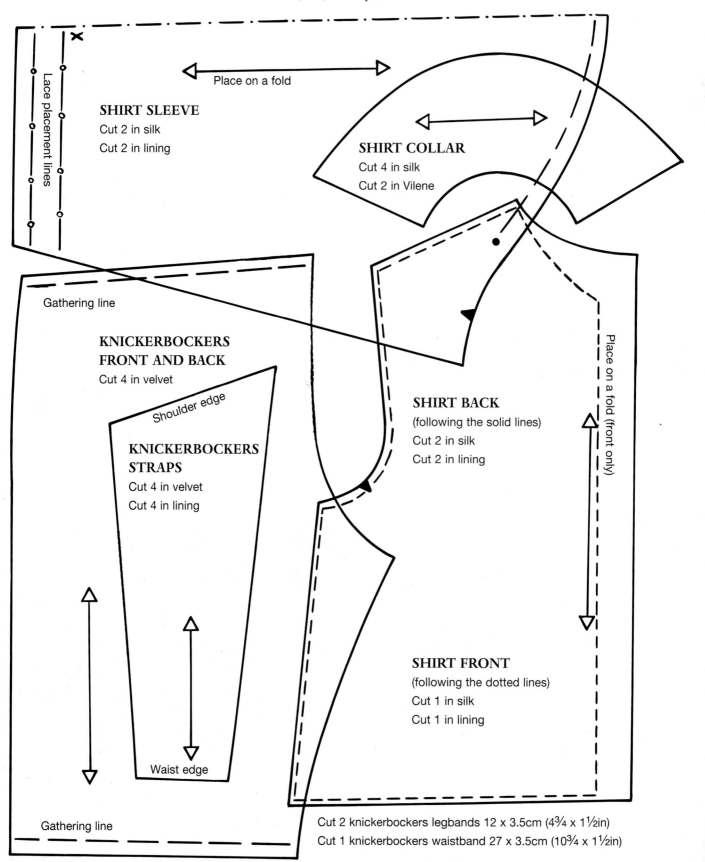

Place on a fold

Lace placement lines

SHIRT SLEEVE
Cut 2 in silk
Cut 2 in lining

SHIRT COLLAR
Cut 4 in silk
Cut 2 in Vilene

Gathering line

KNICKERBOCKERS FRONT AND BACK
Cut 4 in velvet

Shoulder edge

KNICKERBOCKERS STRAPS
Cut 4 in velvet
Cut 4 in lining

SHIRT BACK
(following the solid lines)
Cut 2 in silk
Cut 2 in lining

Place on a fold (front only)

SHIRT FRONT
(following the dotted lines)
Cut 1 in silk
Cut 1 in lining

Waist edge

Gathering line

Cut 2 knickerbockers legbands 12 x 3.5cm (4¾ x 1½in)
Cut 1 knickerbockers waistband 27 x 3.5cm (10¾ x 1½in)